101

Home Office Success Secrets

By
Lisa Kanarek

CAREER PRESS
180 Fifth Avenue
P.O. Box 34
Hawthorne, NJ 07507
1-800-CAREER-1
201-427-0229 (outside U.S.)
FAX: 201-427-2037

101 HOME OFFICE SUCCESS SECRETS
ISBN 1-56414-130-6, $8.95
Cover design by A Good Thing, Inc.
Printed in the U.S.A. by Book-mart Press

To order this title by mail, please include price as noted above, $2.50 handling per order, and $1.00 for each book ordered. Send to: Career Press, Inc., 180 Fifth Ave., P.O. Box 34, Hawthorne, NJ 07507

Or call toll-free 1-800-CAREER-1 (Canada: 201-427-0229) to order using VISA or MasterCard, or for further information on books from Career Press.

Library of Congress Cataloging-in-Publication Data

Kanarek, Lisa.
    101 home office success secrets / by Lisa Kanarek.
        p.   cm.
    Includes index.
    ISBN 1-56414-130-6 : $8.95
    1. Office management.   2. Home-based businesses--Management.   3.
Success in business.   I. Title. II. Title: One hundred one home office
success secrets.   III. Title. One hundred and one home office success
secrets.
    HF5547.K434   1994
    658'.041--dc20
                                                                94-26667
                                                                CIP

DEDICATION

To my husband and best friend, Gary Weinstein.

Contents

Marketing   57

Organization   80

INTRODUCTION

Success is an arbitrary term. Some may define it as money, fame or recognition, while others view it as a feeling of personal satisfaction for a job well done.

In my quest to find and interview 30 successful home office professionals to include in this book, I took several factors into account, including income, length of time in business and business specialty. Two common threads ran throughout these interviews, whether they were conducted in person or over the phone. Each individual expressed a genuine love for what he or she did, and a dedication to working from home.

Many of these home office professionals said they wished they would have started their businesses earlier. Some rediscovered skills that had been buried beneath the agony of a job they no longer found challenging.

A few of the professionals I interviewed originally started working in outside offices because they feared they would not be taken seriously if they worked from their homes. Eventually, they moved their offices home and swore they would never go back. Others never considered an office outside of their home for two reasons: rent and commuting. They weren't willing to pay one or do the other.

The enthusiasm these professionals showed for their businesses was contagious. After each interview, I felt inspired to reevaluate what I was doing and explore ways to improve my own business. I would finish each interview thinking about the exciting and challenging way each person spent his or her day, only to begin another interview that left me feeling the same way.

The goal of this book is to provide you with 101 tips that go beyond the standard way of doing business. The standards have been covered in other business books.

Some tips come directly from these 30 home office professionals, while others represent a compilation of several. These successful home office professionals range from entrepreneurs to corporate employees who work from home.

I have also included organizing tips that are a continuation of tips from my first book, *Organizing Your Home Office for Success.*

As in my first book, I am not so naive as to assume that you will read this book from cover to cover (although I wish you would), but I'm being realistic. Find the tips that apply to you or interest you, read them carefully and determine how you may apply them to your own situation.

I invite you to explore with me the experiences and wisdom of these successful home office professionals. You may hear yourself saying a few "aha's," "I thought so's" and "Why didn't I think of that's!" In addition, you'll discover new ideas, methods for fine-tuning existing ones and inspiration to experiment with others.

CUSTOMER SERVICE

Tip #1

Do Business With a Personal Touch

Some people become so preoccupied with the day-to-day operations of their businesses that they forget to do something special for their clients. If you assume that your clients are happy and that they'll automatically call you if they need anything, think again. This is not always true.

As your client base continues to grow, it is imperative that you maintain the same level of service that you provided when you first earned your clients' business. Then search for the *extra* something to do for them.

For some clients, your basic service is enough, while others want special treatment, even though they may not tell you. The special treatment doesn't have to be expensive or time-consuming. It just has to come from your heart.

Case in point:

Stock in a greeting card company might be a wise investment for Terri Murphy, a speaker, writer and real estate specialist. She thinks nothing of sending more than 800 birthday cards to her clients each year. She writes each card by hand. She enjoys working with her clients and isn't afraid to show them how much. Murphy believes that little things can mean so much.

When it comes to the holidays, however, she skips the cards and sends "Murphy's Law" calendars. Her clients enjoy receiving them, and Terri's photo and phone number on the calendars serve as a visual reminder that she is always ready to help them.

Terri's method of doing business has earned her a reputation of being efficient yet caring, professional yet sensitive to her clients' needs. She works long hours and is available to her clients around the clock. They know that if they need anything she will help them as much as she can, and will do it with a personal touch.

Tip #2

When Working With Clients, Devote Yourself 100% to Them

One of Murphy's Laws has to be, the moment you leave your office, the phone rings. You can be in your office all morning and the only calls you receive come from someone asking you to switch your long-distance service, or someone who misdialed your number.

If you know that likelihood exists, it can be difficult for you as a home office professional, to resist checking your voice mail, answering machine or calling your office. When working with a client, you owe the client your undivided attention. Certainly you want to be accessible to other clients. However, when you're working with a client, the others need to wait.

If you know that you will be out of your one-person office all day, leave a message on your machine or voice mail that clearly states when you will return calls. When you take your mind off your messages, you can focus on your client.

Even if you wear a beeper, unless you expect an extremely urgent call, turn it off. It serves as a distraction that sends a signal to your client that you are only partially with them. In this age of quality customer service, this one action can go a long way toward building a solid working relationship.

Case in point:

"Be here now...be where you are," serves as the motto that Jane Applegate, syndicated columnist and radio commentator, follows religiously. When she is working with a client, she does not return phone calls unless they are absolutely urgent. By following this credo, she reduces her stress and can commit herself entirely to her client.

Applegate's nonstop schedule of speaking, writing, broadcasting and consulting, requires constant focus.

Her willingness to concentrate on her clients has led to long-term contracts with major corporations.

Tip #3

Promote Your Clients' Business

When you work with clients for a long time, you may become so closely tied to their business that you forget that not everyone is familiar with them. If you believe they are the best at what they do, share this.

Tell people with whom you come in contact about your clients, and how they may help others. Someone may have been looking for a certain type of company, yet may never have known it existed.

Some companies promote their clients through radio and television advertisements. The ads usually have two parts. The first part describes the client's company and the second demonstrates how the advertiser helps the client. You can take the same approach on a smaller scale by including mention of a client in your brochure or other sales materials.

Case in point:

When speaking with Barry J. Farber, author of *State of the Art Selling* and president of Farber Training

Systems, Inc., don't be surprised if he tells you something about his own clients and what they can do to
help you. When speaking with others, Farber never
hesitates to recommend his clients' services. When he
believes in what someone else is doing, he is not shy
about sharing the information with others.

Farber believes in giving people more than they expect. They rarely will be disappointed and will appreciate your extra efforts.

When acquiring a new client, Farber knows the new
client will not expect him to be a mouthpiece for the
business, especially because he is under no obligation to
give that company exposure. When he *does* refer his
new clients to others, they're pleasantly surprised.

Farber is always searching for ways to promote his
clients' businesses. In turn, his clients are pleasantly
surprised to see him go out of his way to increase their
businesses through promotion.

Keep your voice mail or answering machine message to
less than one minute. Long-distance callers will appreciate it,
as will local callers who won't have to wait a long time to
leave a message. If callers only have one minute to leave a
message, share that information on your outgoing message. If
you use an answering service, ask the operators to say their
first name after they answer the phone with your company
name. It sounds more professional and may even sound as if
your assistant is answering the phone.

Tip #4

Stay Out of Your Clients' Territory

Did you ever take note of the way that two animals peer into each others' eyes, carefully scrutinizing each other and determining who has trespassed into whose territory? You may be encroaching on your clients' territory without your knowledge. You are or should be working toward mutually beneficial goals and the method for attaining your goals should be beneficial to all.

Until you have worked with clients for awhile and set boundaries, either formal or informal, it is important to know your territory—how to stay off your clients' turf and stay within your own.

Your contact at a company, possibly the owner, may not be aware of everyone's job responsibilities. After all, titles can be ambiguous. When you're given a project, make sure the person with whom you will work does not feel threatened because you're handling something that falls under his or her responsibilities.

Case in point:

Knowing when to avoid crossing her clients' paths keeps Mary Cowart's services in demand. As an independent meeting planner and owner of Mary Cowart

Meeting Consultants, she knows when to back off. Cowart observes the politics within a corporation and gingerly proceeds with any projects she needs to handle. If she thinks she may be crossing into someone else's job responsibility, she backs off.

Cowart has strong working relationships with her clients, yet realizes that if she goes into a client's territory, she could automatically raise a wall between herself and the company. She avoids that by being sensitive to her clients' emotional needs and knowing when to back off.

Tip #5

Pay Attention to What Your Customers Want

Day after day, you may receive dozens of phone calls asking for the same thing. It may be a product or service that you don't currently offer and have never considered offering. What some people call a nuisance, others call a golden opportunity.

Successful businesses have sprouted from a good idea, shaped in the form of a request. Other businesses doing marginally well, have taken off after the owners listened to customers' requests and gave customers what they wanted.

Of course, not all requests are reasonable or even feasible. The ones that are both deserve your full attention. If, for example, you present seminars for your livelihood and people randomly call you requesting audio or video tapes of your programs, you can continue to tell them you don't have any—or create tapes. When making that decision, cost and return on investment will play a large role in the outcome.

Because you are so closely tied to your product or service, it may take an outsider to see how you can improve what you are currently offering. Maybe you have a product available in only one color or size, while customers would welcome a smaller size and an array of colors. You could pre-sell the product, then produce the product, minimizing your risk. Your clients would be happy and so would your business account.

It is easier to maintain the status quo and continue to do business as usual, instead of taking a chance on a new product or service. If, however, the people holding the purse strings want additional products or services, do everything you can to give them what they want. Only a few of your customers may have suggested these ideas to you, yet if you surveyed your other clients, you might find that they, too, would use the product or service if it were offered to them.

Tip #6

Don't Promise What You Can't Deliver, and Don't Deliver Late

The lure of a huge corporation and its seemingly large budget may cause you to make promises you may not be able to keep. Before you say yes to a request, be realistic. Carefully evaluate your current schedule and determine if you have time to complete the job. Don't forget to consider if you are even the right person to handle the project.

Case in point:

Knowing his time limitations has kept Bob LeVitus, author of *Dr. MacIntosh*, busy with projects he enjoys and clients with whom he likes to work. Each time he receives a call from a prospect, he takes a close look at his calendar while, at the same time, scrutinizing his list of ongoing projects.

LeVitus wants to accommodate new clients, yet knows that if he is unable to do a good job because of a time crunch, the client will not be a long-term one. When setting delivery and completion dates, he always builds in a cushion of several days to ensure that he delivers what he promises, when he promises it.

He stresses that even if the most qualified person is available for a job, yet unable to meet a clients' requests, the qualified professional is at a total disadvantage.

He notes that as a contributing editor for *MacUser*, he has little flexibility when it comes to article deadlines. In that situation, skill is not going to overcome a missed deadline. If he has promised an article and is unable to deliver it, the magazine will find someone else to write it. Although that person may not be the magazine's first choice, LeVitus's inability to deliver the article will leave the editors scrambling. Technology plays a major role in speeding up the transmission of an article via modem. He has seen writers frantically transmitting articles at the last minute and knows the message that person is sending: *unprofessional*.

Tip #7

Make It Easy for People to Do Business With You

Your product or service may be irresistible and guaranteed to save others time, money and aggravation. Instead of people beating a path to your door, however, you may have inadvertently set up roadblocks.

How easy is it for people to do business with you? Do you have convenient hours? Not everyone works 9-to-5 every day. Some work late hours and weekends, making it impossible for them to visit your home office or call you when you are available. Be willing to call them after hours or meet with them at their convenience.

Have several clients asked if you offer free delivery? If enough people ask about delivery, include it in your service and build it into your cost, or charge extra for it. If someone has the choice between driving out of their way for something and having it delivered, the client will often opt for the delivery.

Do you miss several phone calls throughout the day? Consider hiring a part-time person to answer your phones or employ an answering service. Voice mail is always an option, but sometimes people like to hear a live voice and feel skittish about leaving messages. You can instruct the answering service to answer the phone any way you like. Many callers will think that they are speaking to a staff person.

Would you double your orders if you had a toll-free number? Surprisingly, you may be losing orders because your competitor offers toll-free calls.

Are you inflexible? When your customers ask for something—for example, an additional service or a product in a different color—do you consider their requests? Keep in mind that if you don't, eventually someone else will. Giving credence to your clients' requests could increase your profits and may spark another business idea.

Tip #8

Work to Communicate at Every Level

Periodically, the plot of a movie will center around someone thinking about buying a business, taking an entry-level position within a company to understand its inner-workings. By disguising his or her identity, the potential owner or president is treated as fairly or unjustly as everyone else.

The moral is to treat everyone the same. You never know...the person you just snubbed may soon replace your client's current contact.

Case in point:

With a client base ranging from the very famous to the not-so-famous, and subcontractors ranging from carpet-layers to carpenters, interior designer Sharon Sistine has developed the ability to communicate in the same way with everyone she meets. Being a phony is not part of her makeup, and she gives her clients the respect they deserve, while treating the subcontractors she uses on the job with the same respect.

One of her clients, a European man, hired her to decorate his home. While working on the home, she had no idea that he was wealthy and famous until she read an article about her client in a business publication. He was low-key about his wealth and appreciated her treating him the same as everyone else. He subsequently hired her to decorate other homes he owned around the country.

Sistine treats the subcontractors with whom she works with the same dignity. She would never dream of speaking down to them in front of a client. If she has a problem with the job they are doing, she discusses it with them alone.

Her subcontractors know that she refuses to let any of her clients "get burned" and, if she feels that a subcontractor has charged a client unfairly, she will pay the difference out of her own pocket. She will also refuse to work with that subcontractor again.

Sistine believes that how you treat people stays with you, and she works to communicate with everyone at the same level.

Tip #9

Look for Other Ways to Serve Existing Clients

When your business is on an upswing and you have more orders than you can fill or more requests for your services than time to fulfill them, the last thing on your mind is how to sell *more*. On the other hand, if you're waiting for the phone to ring and long overdue invoices to be paid, your thoughts will undoubtedly revolve around sales.

Studies have shown repeatedly that it is less expensive to serve an existing client than to market to a prospect. With the latter, you may notice a rise in your phone bill, printing budget and postage costs. Instead of believing that you have exhausted all of your avenues with a client, ask yourself if there is a road you haven't explored.

Case in point:

Knowing that his clients may see his products for only one purpose, Jim Halt with Jostens, an awards and recognition company for the scholastic, industrial and sports industries, constantly devises ways to serve his clients. As a sales consultant in the recognition division, his clients may think that he is limited to providing them with awards. He rectifies that misconception quickly by providing them with new ways to use his products.

Halt begins by talking with his clients about their company goals, then searches for ways to help them achieve those goals. One company that was purchasing sales awards from him started a safety campaign after they realized the staggering costs associated with the firm's lack of safety rules. His client casually mentioned the new direction to Halt, and he quickly devised a safety award program. His client was thrilled with the program and Halt was a hero.

Halt firmly believes that if he counted on his clients to create other means for using his products, his sales would flounder. He realizes that awards are not the top priority of his clients, yet, if he can help his clients find ways to use awards to their benefit, Halt will also benefit by making additional sales.

Tip #10

Be a Resource to Your Clients

When you work with a client, you offer a particular service or product or a variety of services and products. If a client has a request that is outside your area of expertise, recommend someone else. This may not be part of your contract, but your willingness to help will be appreciated. Even if you don't have someone immediately in mind, there is usually someone who knows *someone* who can help you.

Case in point:

Referral is not in Patricia Kaufman's list of services, yet it is an integral part of her business. As an independent insurance broker with a majority of retirees as her clients, she never hesitates to provide them with the names they need.

Kaufman considers her clients her family, and refers them only to companies to whom she would refer her own family. She constantly looks for new businesses to help her clients. Whether she recommends a bill-paying service or home health care provider, she knows that service will treat her clients well.

Since she does not use these services for her own purposes, she seeks feedback from the clients who have used these services to ensure that the companies she recommends provide quality service.

Tip #11

Guard Your Reputation: You Only Lose It Once

If you only have one chance to make a first impression, how many chances do you have to repair a bad reputation? Unfortunately, not many. First impressions fade over time, yet a bad reputation stays with you until you have an opportunity to vindicate yourself, and that opportunity may never come.

Case in point:

With a keen eye for detail and, in the back of her mind, the possibility of a tarnished reputation, Robin Johnson of Vidalia Associates, a market research and strategic communications consulting firm, works to maintain the solid reputation that she and her partner have worked so hard to earn.

Many of Johnson's clients are referrals from other clients. That makes her even more committed to doing an outstanding job for her new clients. If she looks good, the referring client looks good, too.

Johnson doesn't cut corners when she works on a project. The extra money she would pocket by skimping is far less than the money she would lose by doing a bad job and possibly losing a client. If, for example, she hires an inexpensive freelancer to enter data for her, the freelancer may charge Johnson less per hour, yet perform poorly and delay the project. This puts Johnson in the awkward position of scrambling to find someone to repair the damage or risk harming her reputation.

A tarnished reputation will not only affect one client, it will affect others. Johnson works with several clients who own different companies, yet serve on the same board of directors. Johnson knows that if she botches a job with one company, it will cause a ripple effect and spread to other companies.

Tip #12
Make People Feel Good

On the outside, some people appear confident, self-assured and able to handle anything. On the inside, they may feel differently. If you look past the mixture of emotions, feelings and values confined within, you may see an empty place no one has touched. It may take only a kind word or sincere compliment to fill that void.

Look for something that a person does well, a hobby that person enjoys or an area of expertise and ask about it. So often, people may focus on themselves and not make an attempt to connect with someone else. A few words shared with someone else can make a big difference to them and completely turn their day around.

Case in point:

Making people feel good about themselves is easy for Shirley Hutton, the number-one national sales director for Mary Kay Cosmetics. When she meets with clients, she takes it upon herself to change their mood for the better and find something for which they can be happy.

The key to her success in making others feel better about themselves is her sincerity. She fully understands that if she falsely compliments someone, she not only damages her credibility, she stands to ruin the relationship she has worked to develop.

Her high six-figure salary attests to the fact that she knows how to make her customers, and the 350 directors she manages, feel good. If they feel good, she feels even better.

Tip #13

Don't Let Your Hair Down Completely

You may have friends you've known since the first grade, while most friends you've made as an adult. There is another type of friend—the one who is also a client. The way you act around a client should be determined by how you know that client. If the person was a friend first, then a client, you can be yourself. If, on the other hand, the person was a client first, and is now a friend, when you step outside of a business setting, remain professional at all times.

When you are away from your office, you still represent your company. If, while out with a client, you do something reckless, thoughtless or embarrassing, it reflects poorly on you. A friend not associated with your business may laugh it off, while a client may file it in the back of his or her mind and retrieve it during business hours.

If a client notices you doing something inappropriate, your client may wonder if you are handling his or her account the same way. A client may lose faith in your ability to make good decisions.

Case in point:

Having a wide range of friends is important to Lynn Armstrong, of LA Enterprises, a promotional products firm. She knows when to draw the line, however, when her friends are also her clients.

Armstrong has a good time when she is with her clients outside of business hours, yet she doesn't completely let her hair down. She emphasizes that they are indeed her friends while, at the same time, her clients, meaning she must act appropriately. She treats them the way she treats any other friend. However, she is keenly aware that something she does in her personal life can affect her business relationships.

Tip #14

Keep Personal Information Private

America's obsession with the personal lives of others explains the proliferation of tabloid TV, tell-all books and exploitative magazines. These media pry into others' personal lives and share their findings with the world. Editors and publishers justify these exposures, even ruining others' lives, by saying they are just doing their jobs. What if you are exposed to personal information about your clients? Is part of your job to tell others what you know, or to respect your clients' privacy?

Case in point:

Keeping secrets is an important part of Sharon Sistine's business. As an interior designer, she is exposed to her clients' personal lives on a regular basis. She literally knows what people have hidden in their closets.

Sistine's clients include well-known movie stars, millionaires and CEOs of major corporations. Many value their privacy and know that Sistine will respect their wishes.

In dealing with individuals' personal tastes, she realizes that some couples will disagree throughout the decorating process. In these situations, she turns into a therapist, working with each partner to help the couple resolve the problem that is keeping them from making any decisions. She could rush back to her office and tell her friends what she witnessed. Instead, she keeps the information to herself and moves on to other clients.

Sistine is often interviewed by mainstream and trade publication reporters. During these interviews, she could drop a few famous names, yet she refrains and merely mentions the types of clients with whom she has worked. When writers ask her if she has any clients whose houses they can photograph, Sistine knows which clients will accept the idea and which will readily decline. Some are so private that they will not even allow her to photograph their homes for use in her portfolio.

Sistine knows that divulging her clients' personal idiosyncrasies, decorating budget or marital difficulties can only serve to discredit others and make new clients wonder what she is saying about them. Her clients feel comfortable that even though Sistine knows more about them than their close friends, any personal information is safe with her.

Tip #15

Go the Extra Mile for Your Clients

Once you come to an agreement, close a deal and sign a contract, the next step is up to you. You can complete the contract as promised and move on to other clients, or you can provide added touches to the project.

Enhancing your product or service does not always involve money. Your time is a valuable commodity, and by giving some of it, you can improve your status with your client and prove that you are willing to provide more.

Case in point:

Going the extra mile and doing more than his clients expect differentiates Tim Basham's services from his competitors'. As president of Advertising Services And Promotions (ASAP), he routinely looks for ways to increase the value of his services and products.

He recalled a time when one of his major clients had placed a large order for a specialty product to be given as gifts to its clients. His supplier delivered the order to him only one day before his client needed it. With little time to spare, Basham delivered the gifts to his client and spent the entire day helping the staff wrap the gifts and prepare them for delivery.

His client was so impressed with Basham's dedication to the project, that the client placed a larger order the next week. Basham had exceeded his client's expectations and was handsomely rewarded for his efforts.

Basham has never felt comfortable with just "taking the order and walking away." He wants his clients to feel that he is more than an order-taker, that he is someone who can help them meet their goals.

> ### Tip #16
> # Avoid Doing Business With Friends and Relatives

Inevitably, when you least expect it, you will receive a call from a friend or relative asking for your services. At this point, you have three choices. You could charge your normal rate, offer a discount or turn down the business altogether.

If you have ever committed to doing something for a friend or relative, and later regretted it, you may want to choose the third alternative. Often, this situation is like holding a candle to a gas heater. Something is bound to explode.

Case in point:

Being diplomatic about turning down business from friends and family has kept Vicky Mayer's personal relationships intact.

Her specialty, marketing communications for health care businesses, and her skills remain in demand. If her family or friends call to ask for her services, she politely tells them that she appreciates their call. She then explains her business policy.

Mayer admits that she has angered a few friends, yet realizes that agreeing to do business with them is not worth the possibility of losing a friend. She feels that working with family or friends is time-consuming, aggravating and simply not worth it.

This policy has helped her husband out of uncomfortable situations when his friends have asked for her help. He simply reiterates her policy and avoids offending anyone.

Anyone who has agreed to do business with a friend or relative, and grumbles throughout the process, can appreciate Mayer's policy.

MANAGING YOUR OFFICE

Tip #17

While In Your Home Office, Your Home Is Elsewhere

Working from home requires discipline and a bit of imagination. When you work within a corporate setting, the cubicles, offices and copy room set the tone of a work environment. Within a home office, the lack of physical reminders of a work setting, may make it harder to remember that you're at work.

When you work in your home office, treat it as you would an outside office. There, you wouldn't run to the refrigerator every 30 minutes, or throw in a load of laundry between phone calls. Avoid doing household chores during working hours. Soon, you'll be stepping away from the phone or computer to wash up the lunch dishes or reorganize your closets. Eventually, you'll have to make time between your household activities to actually work.

Case in point:

The playful laugh of a young daughter and the nursery rhymes she sings could have been a distraction for Vicky Mayer if she hadn't made alternate arrangements.

Mayer, head of V.W. Mayer, a marketing communication business, has learned how to work in her home office while still raising her daughter. She enlisted the help of a nanny. Mayer counts on the nanny to keep her child entertained while she meets with clients and conducts business in her customized home office.

Mayer knows that a nanny is a temporary arrangement until her daughter goes to school all day. Mayer enjoys the freedom of her own business, yet knows that it takes discipline to work each day instead of stopping to attend to her daughter every few minutes, though she would like to do this.

She stays in her home office during working hours when she is not meeting with her clients, and avoids the areas where her daughter plays until she can take a break.

This arrangement allows her to treat her home office the way she would a corporate office, and remain productive throughout the day.

Tip #18

Invest In Quality Equipment the First Time

The old saying "You get what you pay for" still holds true. There are times when you can get something for a low price and proudly use the product for years. At other times, the bargain product can constantly remind you of a bad deal each time it breaks down.

Before you spend any of your money on new equipment or on modifying your existing equipment, consider a few questions.

1. Will the new item pay off in time saved by using it?

2. Can you afford it or will you have to settle for a less expensive, less effective model? If possible, wait until you can afford the higher model. You will save in the long run.

3. Do you know how to use the equipment? If it is going to take you six months to learn how to use new equipment on your own, be willing to pay someone to teach you how to use it immediately.

A frequently overlooked item is a file cabinet. They are often on sale at irresistibly low prices—but don't be deceived by the price. A lower-priced cabinet will initially cost you less money, but it will eventually wear out. After you have replaced it several times, you will have spent as much as you would have on a higher quality cabinet.

The same is true for an office chair. It may seem insignificant to spend time selecting the right chair. Yet, if you spend a majority of your time in your office, you will appreciate the extra amount you spent selecting a comfortable and functional chair.

Make sure that you avoid wasting time and money by taking the time to find the right equipment and being willing to pay the price.

Tip #19
Partnerships: Establish a Fair System of Compensation

Partnerships offer a plethora of opportunities to all parties involved, from those with varied skills to others with unlimited resources. When forming a partnership, the percentage of work that each party contributes to the company, and the amount of money each earns, are important considerations.

A partnership where two parties contribute equally, yet in different areas, means the division of money is destined to become an issue. As partners, before you obtain your first client, determine what your fee arrangement will be. With that issue clarified, you will be able to focus on your clients' needs instead of your bank account.

Case in point:

Robin Johnson of Vidalia Associates splits her profits equally with her partner, Meg Fitzgerald, thus choosing to go against what attorneys refer to as "eating what you kill." Vidalia Associates could have opted for a system whereby each partner kept what she earned, yet Johnson saw it as more of a disadvantage than an advantage.

She wanted to avoid introducing unnecessary competition into their new working relationship. Johnson and her partner discovered that their monetary and business goals were similar and they didn't want to set up barriers to achieve those goals. If one partner earned more than the other, one would eventually feel slighted and possibly less motivated to work.

Johnson works with her partner on various projects, yet when a particular project calls for her specialty instead of her partner's, Johnson spends more time with the client. If they followed the "eat what you kill" system, Johnson would earn all the profits from the project, leaving her partner with nothing. Her justification for the equal split is that when she is working on a project, her partner is marketing their business, thus contributing in her own way. With this arrangement, they focus on competing with other companies, not each other.

> Keep a stacking tray or wicker tray next to your computer for information you need to enter. This can include paid bills, addresses and notes from client meetings. Empty the tray at least once each week.

Tip #20

Be Willing to Pay
for Quality Staff

As your business grows and the amount of time you have to spend on administrative tasks diminishes, you may want to consider adding staff.

If you want to pay someone minimum wage, yet expect the quality of a salaried employee, remember the old saying, "You get what you pay for."

You have an option to pay a person what he or she is worth, or bring in someone at a lower rate who needs to be trained. There are advantages and disadvantages to both. A skilled professional will minimize the time you spend training. A professional may bring ideas and systems to your business that had not occurred to you. Your close ties to your business could give you a distorted view, and a fresh view from an outsider could give you the extra push you need. The disadvantage is that person may have bad habits that have to be "unlearned."

An unskilled employee gives you the opportunity to train the person to your specifications. Because the unskilled do not have extensive business experience, they should not have bad habits that need to be broken. The disadvantage is that they will require more training and patience from you.

If you want to avoid the inconvenience of training, office politics and tax requirements, consider hiring freelancers to handle certain projects. You can use a graphic artist to design brochures, sales sheets or hand-outs, instead of bringing in an employee. A freelance secretarial service can give you the time you need to handle more pressing matters.

The rule of thumb? Ask yourself what your time is worth. If paying someone to do something that will take you several hours is less than the amount of money you can generate during that time, give the task to someone else.

Case in point:

Lucille Sanchez Pearson, president of Global Resources Ltd., a research firm for management recruitment, knows the value of hiring quality staff. Although she takes time to train everyone she hires, Sanchez knows the value of her time and how much money she will lose if she has to spend hours training someone who will ultimately be unable to handle the job.

Although Pearson seeks out top-notch employees to represent her company, she leaves nothing to chance. She prepares scripts for each employee to use during sales calls. Pearson wants each person working for her to have a concise and clear picture of her company's message. The result of her maintaining high standards when hiring is a low turnover rate. This allows Pearson to spend more time selling than training.

Tip #21

Don't Hire Friends

Friends may come and friends may go. You may find them going faster than you anticipate if you hire them. It is one thing to be a friend, discussing world events, the latest trends and even other friends. It is an entirely different and, for many, alien experience to turn a friend into an employee.

Before you make the decision to include a friend in your business, ask yourself a few questions.

1. Will I be able to tolerate this person for eight hours each day?
2. Does he or she fit the image of my company?
3. Is he or she personable, thus giving my company a good name?
4. If things don't work out, will I be able to fire him or her?
5. Will he or she be able to separate our personal life from our working relationship?

Case in point:

Amy Dacyczyn, publisher and author of *The Tight-wad Gazette,* learned the hard way that hiring friends is a bad idea. When she started her business three years ago, she didn't want to spend more than she had to on staff (a true and smart tightwad), so she hired a friend.

At the time, this seemed to be a good idea. When she eventually realized that her friend was better suited as a friend than an employee, Dacyczyn found it hard to fire her. She had mixed feelings about hurting her friend, but didn't want to sacrifice the quality of her business. She finally fired the friend and has managed to salvage the friendship.

Dacyczyn's business and friendships are equally important to her, which is why she keeps the two separate.

Tip #22
Kick Your Staff Out of Your Office

The old image of an office was of a boss standing over his employees, badgering them to work harder. Such behavior resulted in an office filled with employees suffering from stress, intimidation and resentment. Employees processed mounds of paperwork, compiled reports and completed projects as quickly as possible to appease the boss for the moment.

Fortunately, advances in technology have replaced the archaic offices of the past, and have opened new avenues for operating businesses without a full staff in the same office. These new offices have been called "virtual offices" and "offices without walls." They are as effective as offices filled with employees and allow each person to work at his or her own pace, while still being aware of others' activities.

Case in point:

Through trust, ingenuity and technology, Terry Brock, president of Achievement Systems, Inc., a company that trains individuals and businesses to use computers and technology, runs his business alone—with the help of others. He used to have a staff in his office in Norcross, Georgia, answering calls, fulfilling requests and keeping his office open while he traveled out of town working with clients. One day he realized that he needed his staff, but not in his office.

His office manager, whose home office is in Montana, keeps Brock's office running smoothly, even though they rarely meet face-to-face. She handles his desktop publishing and mails materials from her home office. They communicate via voice mail, fax and modem. Brock knows that his office manager is doing her job and that he doesn't need to be in the same office with her to ensure that projects are accomplished. She has the ability to get the job done because of the technology available to her. If he needs additional help, he has resources in Seattle and New York.

Tip #23

Buying Computer Equipment Is Like Shooting at a Moving Target

---

Modern technology is both exciting and intimidating. Computer companies continually tout the latest technology guaranteed to make life easier. At the point you finally decide which computer system to buy, manufacturers introduce a new model. You can play the waiting game when considering a computer purchase, or play the game of chance. You can best win the computer game if you determine what you need a computer to do before you buy it.

As you walk down the aisles of your local computer store, don't search for the perfect system at the perfect price. Before you make the purchase, do you inevitably ask the question, "Should I wait for the next model?" If you attempt to keep up with everyone else and own the computer that is this year's rage, instead of what you truly need, you will waste time and money.

Case in point:

Bob LeVitus, contributing editor for *MacUser* and author of *Dr. Macintosh,* advises his readers to realize that buying the right computer equipment equals shooting at a moving target. There is always going to be a new computer that is faster and able to do more. Rather than wait for the next computer, make the jump when you need a new computer.

As new computers are introduced, the prices of the older models (a relative term in the computer world) will drop. Instead of buying the latest model, consider the model below it and eventually upgrade to the next model. During his seminars, LeVitus demonstrates the various features of a computer and how to make the computer do more for you. Don't become determined to buy a completely new system when what you have could be easily updated.

When using a contact manager software program, use a "dump page" to store phone numbers that you may have reason to use, yet not necessarily. If, for example, someone calls you to request pricing information, you can record their phone number and address on the dump page. In case you ever need the number again, you know where to find it.

Tip #24

When You Receive Your First Payment From a Client, Copy the Check

When you work with new clients and feel unsure of their stability or payment habits, you have many choices. You can make a credit check, demand full or partial payment in advance or take your chances.

Depending upon your cash flow situation, the first two options may be more viable. If a client feels insulted by your request for either one, consider that a red flag and weigh your options again. It is impossible to predict the events that may happen between the time you acquire the client and when you finish the project. During that period, the client may have lost his or her best account or salesperson to a competitor, putting a crimp in the cash flow.

Not knowing what could happen to a client, especially a new one, warrants certain precautions.

Case in point:

Vicky Mayer of V.W. Mayer, takes a nontraditional approach, following the advice of a friend, and always copies the front and back of the first payment she receives from a client. She wants to know the bank and account information in case she does not receive future payments. By having these numbers, she can take steps to freeze the company's account.

Fortunately, Mayer hasn't had to use the account numbers, yet she feels this precaution may serve her well in the event that she encounters a nonpaying or slow-paying client.

Mayer has a surefire way to avoid nonpayment altogether. If she has a bad feeling about someone, she doesn't do business with them. This is advice that you may tend to ignore when the lure of a new account hooks you.

Tip #25

Keep Your Office
In Your Office

When you worked in a corporate office, your storage space probably was limited to your office or cubicle and any other rooms that were designated for storage. At home, your storage space can easily go from your office, to your basement, to your garage and attic. Before you know it, you may consider adding on to your home or investing in an outside storage shed to hold more "stuff."

Instead of spreading everything throughout your home, set limits. Pack rats don't like to hear this, but you must be realistic about what you keep. Store anything related to your business in your office, rather than scattering it throughout your home. If your office is bursting with information, supplies and products, designate another closet or portion of your home to storage. Don't go overboard and turn every empty space into a storage annex. The more places you have to look for something, the more likely you are to end your search empty-handed.

If you use a spare bedroom or guest room as your office, convert the closet into storage space for files, supplies and reference materials. Take anything out of the closet that is not related to your business (if you have the room) and devote the closet to business supply storage. If you can't spare the entire closet, devote a portion of it to your business.

Case in point

Lucille Sanchez Pearson, president of Global Resources Ltd., a research firm for management recruitment, keeps all of her file cabinets and supplies stored in a large walk-in storage closet. Whenever she needs a reference file (a file she refers to less often than her current files), she opens her closet. By keeping her files in one place, she doesn't waste time looking for information she needs. She doesn't need to leave her office, which would leave her open to distractions throughout her home. She keeps her current files, the ones she uses regularly, near her desk.

Storing her supplies in one place makes shopping for office supplies easy. Pearson never overbuys because she knows what she owns, down to the last paper clip. Her self-contained office helps her to stay focused on what she needs to do at work.

Tip #26

Create a Buffer Between Work and Home

When you worked in a corporate office, the commute to work gave you time to collect your thoughts before you arrived, while the drive home gave you time to unwind. In a home office, the amount of time you save commuting is better spent at work or with your family. The lack of a commute, however, means that you often go directly from your office to your home with no break in between.

Create a buffer between your home life and office life to make the transition between the two easier. You can go to the gym at 5 p.m. each day or tape your favorite program and watch it after work.

Case in point:

David Morgenstern, president of Morgenstern and Partners, an international advertising creative service, takes a daily afternoon walk with his dog. To his neighbors, this activity appears to be part of his exercise regimen. Although his walk keeps him in shape, the true purpose of the exercise is to cool down at the end of the day.

After more than five years in business, Morgenstern discovered that he enjoyed his evening more if he did not go directly "home" after being in his home office all day. Although he values his time with his family, he knows that he is more relaxed at the end of the day if he takes the time to get out of his "work mode" and into his "home mode." When he returns from his walk, he is ready to spend time with his family and discuss the events of the day.

Voice mail can be a quick and efficient way to communicate. There are a few ways to help you use voice mail more efficiently.

When you call someone who has voice mail, write down the extension to bypass the operator or opening message the next time you call.

As you listen to the messages in your voice mail, record them in one place, preferably within your daily planner.

When recording your outgoing message, give callers the option of bypassing your message (if possible).

Tip #27

Set Up Your Office
Where You Want It to Be,
Not Where It Should Be

Working from home offers many advantages. Included among them is the freedom to set up your home office to your liking. Whether you convert your large, sunny family room (congratulations—you finally get a window office!) into your new headquarters or turn a walk-in closet into an organized and efficient office, the choice is yours.

Even if clients will see your office, as long as it's located near an entrance, or the path to your office is relatively clear (your clients will notice if it's a mess), you still have free reign as to where you can set up your office.

However, it's still a good idea to be as practical as possible when choosing the location for your home office. For example, a spare room or basement may seem to be the obvious place for your office, yet it may not be well-lit or it could be too small for you to function in effectively. Keep in mind that if you set up a home office in a place in which you won't want to work, it doesn't matter how functional or well-organized your office is.

Case in point:

Terry Brock, a professional speaker who trains individuals and businesses on the use of computers and technology, has a high-tech, high-nature home office. His office is equipped with the latest in complex technology, yet overlooks a woods and stream.

When you call Brock, don't be surprised to hear birds in the background. He used to be embarrassed by the noise and even thought about moving his office to another room. Although moving would solve the noise problem, losing the view and calm setting wasn't worth it to Brock. Ironically, after awhile his clients started commenting about how nice it must be to work so close to nature. Brock couldn't agree more.

MARKETING

Tip #28

Use Speaking Engagements to Promote Your Business

A national study conducted a few years ago showed that the fear of speaking before a group ranked as the number-one fear in the United States, outranking even the fear of death. Although a few speakers may have died, figuratively speaking, in front of an audience, the benefits of public speaking far outweigh the risks.

You have options in the way you speak before groups. You can present two-hour workshops, or one-hour motivational keynote presentations. Half-day, full-day and multiple-day seminars are other options. The keys to a successful presentation, no matter what the length, are preparation, knowledge and a passion for the information you share.

If the person standing before an audience is not interested in what he or she is saying, this becomes obvious to everyone. In this case, even the presenter shouldn't be there, much less the audience.

When you present a seminar, workshop or keynote, the audience perceives you as an expert. Experts initially command respect, until others believe they know more than the presenter. That won't happen if you do your homework and know your information. Speaking before a group is an inexpensive and profitable way to market your business.

Inexperienced speakers have an ideal opportunity to practice in front of volunteer groups and business clubs. Although you may speak for a reduced fee, or for free, you expose yourself to several opportunities at one time.

You never know—the human resources or training director for a major corporation may be in the audience and hire you afterwards to give a presentation. Or the president of a well-established corporation may refer you to his or her high-powered friends in other corporations.

The audience members may be comprised of persons who hold similar positions, yet they work for different companies. Instead of exposing yourself to one company, you're reaching several at one time.

Case in point:

Telling tales from the trenches of Wall Street keeps audiences intrigued, and Laura Pedersen, a professional public speaker and financial consultant, in demand. She has parlayed her background as the youngest person, at age 22, to hold a partnership in a Wall Street firm, into a successful speaking career that takes her around the country.

To prepare for her multiple speaking engagements to investors and college students, she reads 50 magazines each month. She knows that in the rapidly changing field of finance, she is apt to be asked any number of questions, and she is expected to know the answers.

Pedersen makes the task of scheduling her seminars easier by turning that responsibility over to a speakers' bureau. The bureau gets a percentage of her speaking fee, yet she feels that the time it spends making the arrangements is worth the cost.

Since her speaking keeps her on the road more than 60 percent of the time, she employs a part-time assistant to handle her clients' questions and concerns. She knows her topic not only by studying it, but by living it.

Tip #29

Make All of Your Marketing Materials First-Class

You may work in a state-of-the-art home office, yet your clients may never see it. What they will see, however, is the information generated from within your home office. Make sure that whatever leaves your office is the highest quality you can afford.

Your office furniture does not have to be the best available and your computer does not have to be the latest model. Those items do not necessarily affect your output. A low-quality printer will. A dot matrix printer is a poor substitute for a laser printer. Cut back somewhere else and buy the higher quality printer.

Take a close look at your letterhead and envelopes. Are they printed on a low-grade paper, or on a heavier paper stock? Your business cards don't have to be printed with raised lettering, but the printing should be clean and easy to read.

Are your materials up-to-date? If you move to a new home office or decide to use a postal suite, do not scratch out the old address or put a sticker over the old address. Reprint your letterhead. You can always cut the address off your old letterhead, if it's printed on the bottom, and use the outdated stationery for short notes.

Your image will be reflected in whatever materials you send to clients or prospects. Make every effort to make a positive impression.

Case in point:

Nothing that isn't first-class is allowed to leave the offices of John Osborne, business consultant, investment banker and partner in Osborne Applegate. He won't allow it. He knows that his materials are often the first way prospects have to judge him. He spends what it takes to create the highest quality materials.

Osborne says that even though a professional works out of his or her home, and may be the sole employee, he or she doesn't have to look like it. You can compete with the big companies. You just have to be willing to spend the money for top-quality materials.

Tip #30

Make One Promotional Piece Do More

Printing expenses may often rival both postage and long-distance costs. In your desire to have top-quality promotional materials without having to mortgage your home, be creative.

When designing a postcard, think of several ways it can be used. You can jot quick notes to clients or prospects, or send a reminder throughout the year to your best clients. Design the card so that one side is blank and the other contains a printed message. If you want to mail it, you must have a blank side to write the client's address and your return address. If you want to use the card as an enclosure note, you can write on both sides.

Authors often have extra book covers printed. One side contains the jacket content of their book, and the inside remains blank. You can use the jacket as a promotional vehicle with information about your company printed inside. You can also cut the jacket in half and paste the front cover on a two-pocket folder. Or, fold the book jacket in half and include it in your press packet instead of using the actual book.

A one-page sales sheet can be used in proposals or as the back of a handout you give to audiences when presenting speeches.

Make your letterhead do more than hold letters. Keep the design generic enough to be used for invoices (if you don't have separate forms), news releases or proposal cover sheets.

Your business card can become a mini-brochure. Instead of using a traditional business card, use one with a flap. The front flap can carry a catchy phrase, inside the business card contains your name, company name, address, phone and fax number. The inside flap can include a brief description of your company and services.

Before you print your next sales piece, think of ways that it can serve you. You will be able to invest in a higher quality promotional piece and will not be stuck with thousands of printed materials that you use only occasionally.

Tip #31

Tell Everyone About Your Product

Have you ever stopped to think about the number of places you visit each day? During the week, you may spend a majority of your time in various offices with your clients. On other days, your time may be filled with home office tasks sprinkled with just a few outside errands.

Wherever you go, you have opportunities to showcase your product or services to others. Are you taking advantage of these opportunities or are you letting them slide past you?

Case in point:

Spreading the word about her products is something Shirley Hutton is never afraid of doing. According to Hutton, the number-one national sales director for Mary Kay Cosmetics, "No one has ever crossed my path who I didn't approach." Whether she is in the grocery store or her neighborhood dry cleaner, she is always aware of the people around her, and sees everyone as a potential client.

In a nonthreatening manner, she shares the virtues of her products and gives people ways to enhance their appearance. Hutton is sensitive to others' feelings and if someone is not interested, she graciously backs away. She believes so strongly in her products that she wants others to experience the benefits and is eager to tell them about what's available.

Hutton teaches the 350 directors she supervises the right and wrong way to approach people. They, in turn, pass these techniques on to their sales consultants. She is keenly aware that the wrong approach can anger someone and dissuade them from ever using her products. By being sensitive to their moods and reactions, she continues to interest people in her products.

Tip #32

Teach Classes

An old saying states that those who can, do, and those who cannot, teach. That myth is dead. Those who can, now teach and share their skills with others. In addition to imparting their expertise, the self-employed build their reputations and gain new clients.

Junior colleges and various universities welcome business professionals as teachers of their continuing education courses. Some business people use teaching as a way to supplement their incomes while others view teaching as an ongoing marketing tool. If a business specialist's class is announced in the course catalog each semester, he or she gains exposure to audiences who might otherwise know nothing about the person.

Corporations often turn to continuing education departments for seminar leaders. Corporations bring these instructors into their businesses to train employees. Sometimes the university may impose a referral fee, yet these fees are often reasonable.

Teaching a continuing education course requires no degree. Instead, you need a clear understanding of what you teach and an ability to convey your message clearly and concisely. This is not an eight-week "infomercial" about your company, so be careful to keep your course informative, educational and interesting.

Case in point:

Teaching others the skills that came naturally to CPA Nathan Reeder didn't occur to him until he started his own accounting firm. He approached a junior college and offered to teach accounting courses. After a few classes, many of his students became his clients. They referred him to other clients and his business blossomed.

He knew that teaching at night would take time away from his business and family, yet he also knew that he could increase his client base while helping others with their accounting abilities. As he taught these courses, more people heard about him and inquired about his services and fees.

Do you have too many forms? Before you design another form, ask yourself these questions:

Does a form already exist that would serve the same purpose?

Could I eliminate any forms that I am no longer using?

Could two or three forms be combined to serve several purposes?

If you have a staff, will anyone else in the office use this new form?

Tip #33

Send Memorable Holiday Cards

Beginning around December 12, corporate mailboxes become filled with holiday cards—some funny, some serious, some boring. What makes one card stand out from another? Originality.

Instead of sending a standard card produced by a greeting card manufacturer, design your own. This may cost a bit more, yet the end results will be worth the expense. If you are not artistic, hire someone to handle the design and layout.

Mailing labels work ideally for day-to-day business mailings. When sending holiday cards, take the time to hand-address the cards or hire someone with legible handwriting or even calligraphy skills to address them for you. In addition, take the time to sign each card. You don't have to write a personal message, just add your signature. There is something impersonal about receiving a card engraved with your company name and no signature. It will take time to sign each card, yet your clients will appreciate that extra touch.

There is no rule of thumb that you must send cards in December. You can send Thanksgiving, Valentine's Day or Fourth of July cards. It depends upon your relationship with your clients and your willingness to break out of the corporate mold.

Case in point:

Each year, Art Shay, internationally known photo journalist, creates a new "Happy Everything" card, that highlights a photograph of his greatest achievement of that year. One year, Art posed in front of a collection of his photographs hanging in the National Portrait Gallery.

These unusual greeting cards serve two purposes: First, the cards are not easily forgotten by the recipient, and second, they publicize Shay's achievement. He says that his clients and friends eagerly await each year's cards and attempt to guess what the picture will feature.

Tip #34

Give People the Opportunity to Sample Your Product Properly

As the old saying goes, "You only have one chance to make a first impression." When it comes to people, their looks, actions and words will determine the impression they make. With products, the quality and benefits of using the product are not always apparent. The conditions under which a product is sampled may open doors for you, or slam them in your face.

Attitudes not related to your product, but rather to a person's environment, could influence that person's buying decisions. Someone may be watching the time instead of your presentation. Schedule an appointment with a prospect or client when he or she will not be so pressed for time. If you do not give a client ample time to test your product by rushing his or her decision, the client may reject your product immediately.

Your product or service may be difficult to understand, and if a potential client is unclear about what you are offering, he or she may be too embarrassed to admit it. Pride can stand in the way of a new business relationship that could otherwise be salvaged if you present your product correctly.

It's natural to present the features of a product or service and forget to mention the benefits, even though they may be obvious. By presenting a complete package, including what the client will gain by working with you, you will reach them on different levels.

Case in point:

Believing in her products and knowing how to show them in the best light skyrocketed Shirley Hutton to the top of her field. As the number-one national sales director for Mary Kay Cosmetics for several years in a row, she broke a company record. Before Hutton reached the top position at Mary Kay and was calling on clients, she scheduled appointments with clients during time that she knew she would have a client's full attention. Then she listened to her client's needs and showed the client the right products to meet their needs. Showing her products in the proper way resulted in an avalanche of sales.

She shares her philosophy with the 350 directors who report to her. The result is an increase in their sales figures year after year. Hutton realizes that women have other options when buying skin care products, yet knows that when the products are shown correctly, they will sell themselves.

Tip #35

Send a Business Anniversary Card

Shortly after Thanksgiving, companies and individuals send holiday cards, some preprinted and others handwritten. In the avalanche of mail a few weeks before Christmas, is your card getting lost in the shuffle?

Somewhere, some time ago, someone must have decreed that you had to send your clients cards at the end of the year. What about other special occasions? Why not pull yourself out of the holiday card game—with the exception of clients who would never forgive you—and send business anniversary cards?

Do you remember the first meeting you had with each client? Granted, the date may not stick in your mind, yet if you search, you can find the date written or entered on your calendar. Take the time to note your first official meeting and send a card to celebrate the date.

At first, this tradition may seem odd and even un-businesslike. That's the point. Do you think that your client will ever forget your card? Probably not. If anything, the client will be flattered that you remembered.

You can buy an anniversary card—if you find an appropriate one—or write a note on preprinted, decorative paper. The point is to mark the occasion and let your client know you remembered. In your note or card, let the company know that you are looking forward to working together for many more years.

Tip #36
Practice Relationship Marketing

The old saying, "It's not what you know, it's who you know," could be replaced with, "It's not only who you know, but whether who you know needs your help." Having a network of friends and former business associates can serve as a springboard for your business. Having the nerve to contact these people about your business is the first step.

Case in point:

Robin Johnson and Meg Fitzpatrick, partners in Vidalia Associates, a market research and strategic communications consulting firm, combed their Rolodexes and contacted people they knew. Fitzpatrick, whom Johnson calls a "marketing genius," taught her the profitable skill of relationship marketing—selling to people familiar to you and to people familiar with your qualifications.

At first, Johnson felt uncomfortable with the idea of marketing, especially over the phone. Fitzpatrick convinced Johnson that it would be easier to sell their services to others who knew their capabilities and the high quality of service they would deliver.

The partners talked with colleagues, friends and people with whom they had worked before and searched for ways to help them solve their business problems. Neither partner was overbearing or pushy when they made their phone calls or during their face-to-face meetings. They enjoyed the opportunity to talk with the people on their list and, if the recipient couldn't use the partners' services, they asked for names of people who could.

As a result of their relationship marketing strategy, the partners continue to receive business from the people they initially called and from others those same people have referred.

Tip #37
Slick Isn't Always Better

As your business grows and you get more clients, you may feel added pressure to update your marketing materials (see Tip #29). Having first-class materials is important, yet maintaining the image of your company is even more important.

If you hire a well-known attorney to represent you in a major case, you do not feel surprised to walk into the attorney's spacious waiting room that displays expensive paintings on the wall, coffee served in the finest china and deep leather couches. The office reflects the attorney's image.

If you go to your dentist, you first think about how much a routine checkup will set you back. In this case, a slicker office can send the wrong message.

The same holds true with anything that leaves your office. It must be in keeping with your business.

Case in point:

Knowing how to save money on practically everything remains Amy Dacyczyn's niche. She remains a tightwad even though her business earns six figures and her book, *The Tightwad Gazette,* spent four weeks on *The New York Times* bestseller list.

Her monthly newsletter, "The Tightwad Gazette," hasn't changed in the three years she has published it. She is familiar with desktop publishing, but knows that if she changes the layout and look of her newsletter, she will betray her subscribers' loyalties.

Each month she types and pastes up her newsletter and sends it to the printer. She knows that is what her subscribers expect and she respects their wishes. In her case, a slick look could destroy her credibility as much as if she stopped being a tightwad—something she can't afford to do.

Use postcards with your photo printed on them to send quick notes to prospects and clients. You will save time writing shorter notes on postcards because you won't have to use your letterhead. In addition, your photo will serve as a reminder of who you are, in case the recipient has forgotten.

Tip #38
Publish a One-Page Newsletter

Newsletters are an inexpensive yet effective way to remind your clients and prospects about your products or services. You can publish a newsletter whether you are a real estate agent, accountant, marketing consultant or writer. And your newsletter can impart valuable information that is pertinent to your business—whether it's home fix-it tips, important tax law changes, interesting demographics or anecdotes meant to entertain. The way you write it, lay it out and to whom you send it will determine whether it is read or tossed in the round file.

Case in point:

Alan Caruba, a master newsletter writer, uses newsletters to maintain good relationships with existing clients and open communications with new ones. With three decades of experience as a PR counselor and editorial consultant, Caruba has created many prize-winning newsletters. He offers these tips for starting a newsletter:

1. Develop a mailing list keyed to your long-range plan for markets and services and be sure to keep the list up-to-date. It is better to err on the side of greater outreach than to distribute to a too-small group of companies. It doesn't cost much to print a few more copies.

2. Be brief. People don't have the time or inclination to read long articles these days. Aim for a single sheet or, at most, a four-pager.

3. Emphasize design. Poor layout, artwork and photography will doom your newsletter. A graphic artist is a good investment.

4. Hire a professional writer. Devote your time to determining content, providing data and checking accuracy.

5. Plan for adequate production time. Always begin a newsletter's preparation two months before final publication date. Time is needed to write, design and print it.

6. Keep your newsletter timely. Content must reflect current concerns, not a rehash of old news. Offer predictions and tips to respond to the changing times and challenges ahead.

7. Personalize it. Don't shy away from controversy. Let your newsletter show you have a point of view, expressed in a moderate, reasoned manner.

8. Always include your address, phone and fax.

9. Publish no less than twice a year, and, preferably, quarterly.

10. Where applicable, send copies to appropriate media with permission to quote, increasing the public relations benefits you may receive.

Tip #39

Find an Angle and Focus On It

When your phone rings and it's a prospect asking you for a service you have never offered, your first inclination may be to say yes even though the request is out of your field. Some people justify doing this by saying that they will learn what they can from others and deliver the product or service.

Sometimes this works well, but other times it can backfire. If you commit to something, yet have no idea how you're going to accomplish it, you may not only lose face, you may lose a client.

This doesn't mean that you shouldn't be responsive to your clients' needs. Just be realistic about your abilities. When you do what you know, and know what you're doing, your efforts will be handsomely rewarded.

Case in point:

Finding an angle that some had overlooked, yet others needed, has put money into tightwad Amy Dacyczyn's wallet. She chose to focus on frugality, and set out on a mission to discover what had already been written about the subject. Unsatisfied with what she found, she took a different approach and started publishing her newsletter, "The Tightwad Gazette." As she began to receive media calls from around the country, she soon realized that her newsletter was "the right publication at the right time."

People were struggling to make ends meet, and she had the perfect solutions for them in her monthly newsletter, priced at $12 per year. Dacyczyn figured that if someone saved at least one dollar each month by following the tips in her newsletter, a true tightwad would be willing to part with $12. Readers trusted her advice because she had become a well-known expert on the subject.

She is known as a tightwad and does not pretend to specialize in anything else. When the media thinks of frugality, Dacyczyn wants them to think of her and call her first. They often do.

Tip #40

Mail Clippings, Comics, Etc., to Clients and Prospects

While reading a magazine or the newspaper, you may run across an article or comic strip that applies to a client. Instead of thinking the client has probably seen it, clip it, attach a note (even a sticky note) and send it to the client.

When you do this occasionally (too much paper is overwhelming), your clients will appreciate the extra time you have taken to keep them informed and entertained. Don't waste their time, however. Only send things that will be of value to them.

Sending such information is a good way to get your foot in the door. Later on it serves as an excuse to keep your name in front of them.

Sending articles, comics and other information requires nothing more than a short note. A formal letter typed on your letterhead increases the amount of paper you send and ruins the spontaneity of the gesture. You could print postcards that include your name, phone number and even photo, if you send notes to several prospects. The postcards can double as fax cover sheets to save transmission time.

When you find something to send, yet don't have time to mail it immediately, store it in a file folder labeled "Articles to Send," and keep the folder nearby. Check it at least once each week and mail the information to the appropriate people.

Limit your notes to a few short sentences. A note can read, "Thought you would enjoy this," or "Congratulations on your achievement." The more notes you send, the more proficient you will become at it.

Save the recipient time by highlighting the section or sections you want them to read. Otherwise the client may put it aside and forget to read it, or may miss the point of why you sent the item in the first place.

ORGANIZATION

Tip #41

Grow Into
a Routine

Work schedules can intimidate some, while others function well within certain time constraints. If you work in your home office only when you feel inspired to work, you will either spend a minimal amount of time in your home office or overdose on working hours.

Follow a work schedule as much as possible to keep your productivity high and your motivation strong. You may feel more productive in the morning, so schedule your important tasks for that time. If you feel inspired after lunch to tackle big projects, schedule those tasks in the afternoon.

A phone that rings all day tends to limit the amount of work you complete, unless you screen your calls. Let an answering machine or your voice mail take messages for you. If you need to be available to take calls, start work earlier or resign yourself to working after hours.

Case in point:

Bob LeVitus of *Dr. Macintosh* fame makes every minute in his home office count, by designating certain hours to work in his office,

Each morning by 6 a.m., LeVitus is in front of his computer, hard at work. He stops a few hours later to eat breakfast with his children, sends them off to school, then returns to his office. He stops working at 2 p.m. when his children come home from school, and spends time with them. Sometimes he works after dinner when he is on a tight deadline.

His schedule keeps him focused without making him feel confined. At times, his schedule changes, but for the most part, he works the same hours each day. He considers himself a morning person and arranges his schedule to complete important tasks early in the day.

Tip #42

Realize That Things Take Twice as Long and Cost Three Times as Much

Time and money are valuable commodities. No matter how much you plan ahead by budgeting and scheduling at length, things may not turn out as well as you planned. Budgeting and scheduling, while valuable activities to give you a definite starting point, need to be realistic and flexible.

The person who is unable to deal with the unexpected and unanticipated is doomed to fail. That person will be more concerned with where he or she made the mistake than how to fix it.

Patience is a virtue and, in business, it is a necessity. Even the most detailed plan, broken down to the smallest degree, is subject to changes and situations beyond your control.

Case in point:

Jane Applegate, syndicated columnist and author of *Succeeding In Small Business,* was an overnight success. She claims her success took 20 years to achieve.

She was willing to invest the time to learn about her chosen field and to make valuable contacts along the way. Applegate was realistic about the amount of time certain projects would take to come to fruition. She saved money in areas where she could and put her money where it needed to be.

She now divides her time between writing her syndicated column: *Succeeding In Small Business*, recording a regular radio report, publishing a newsletter and appearing on a weekly CNBC business program.

Is your wallet too full?

Take a few minutes to remove scraps of paper, business cards and other information that you don't need.

Evaluate the credit cards you carry and take out the ones you haven't used in awhile. If you know that you will never use them, destroy them.

Tip #43
Avoid Perfection

Do you take perfectionism too far? Do you work hard each day with minimal results? If so, you may be focusing on doing things right instead of doing the *right things*. Perfectionists appear to be productive on the surface when, in reality, their quest for perfection keeps them from being so. When you recognize the extent of your perfectionism, you will dramatically increase your productivity.

Determine if you spend a majority of your time on top priority items. Perfectionists often focus on tasks they do perfectly, while ignoring those they don't do as well, although they may be more important.

Writing a new sales brochure may not be your strength, yet if you insist on perfection, you'll never finish the brochure. Write an initial draft, then hire someone to help you finish it. A perfectionist takes time to revise a proposal that isn't due for weeks instead of handling an urgent request from a client. He knows that he can handle one task better than another and refuses to work by priority. You'll increase your productivity if you handle top priorities, whether or not the tasks use your strengths.

Your priorities change, so it is important to be flexible whenever possible. Perfectionists experience frustration when things don't work out perfectly. A client may delay a decision about a project, and the delay may alter the rest of the project. This can ruin a perfectionist's day. When you accept that things won't always work out as planned, you can still remain productive.

You may be a perfectionist without realizing it, because perfectionism can blind you to your habits. Here's a clear sign that you are a perfectionist: You rarely feel satisfied with the first draft of anything you do. You may type and retype the same letter or report several times because it isn't perfectly centered on the page or the type style isn't right. This ultimately results in a waste of your time.

There is nothing wrong with striving for perfection (or near-perfection). It becomes a problem when your quest for perfection affects the quality and quantity of the work you produce. Perfectionism may initially open doors for you, because you will be perceived as organized and detail-oriented. Eventually, however, it could close the doors to your success. Striving for increased productivity means working smarter, not harder, and focusing on the end result, thus giving you time to enjoy your success.

Make two sets of photocopies of the front of your credit cards. Store one copy in your safe deposit box and the other in your file cabinet. If you lose your credit cards or are the unfortunate victim of theft, you'll save time searching for the account numbers since they will all be in one place.

Tip #44

Focus On What You've Done, Not What You Haven't Done

To-do lists serve many purposes, such as keeping you focused, or taking a strain off of your memory. Many people use them religiously, while others shun them out of sheer frustration. Those who shun lists often do so because it clearly shows what they could *not* do each day.

Lists don't have to serve as a reminder of tasks yet to be completed, or goals so unattainable that they turn into impossible dreams. A list can serve as a reminder of what you have already done, and motivate you to do more.

Think back to the last list you compiled. Did it give you a clear picture of what you still needed to do or did it highlight those tasks that you completed without fail? What happens when you complete a task? Does someone pat you on the back or break out the champagne and laud you with compliments? If not, why not reward yourself?

Case in point:

When it comes to celebration, Ann McGee-Cooper, consultant and author of *You Don't Have To Go Home From Work Exhausted!* and *Time Management For Unmanageable*

People is the master. She knows the value of rewarding good behavior, even her own. At the end of the day, she writes what she calls a "celebration list."

She recommends the following for making your celebration list. On a blank sheet of paper, or in a section of your daily planner, list everything you accomplished, no matter what priority. It may be an urgent task that you completed in record time with little or no stress, or a small, meaningless task that has been gnawing at you for some time.

McGee-Cooper stresses that no task is too small to add to your list. If you did it, celebrate! She considers a celebration list a motivator for future tasks. There is no need to wait for that pat on the back. Reach back, give yourself a pat on the back and add that task to your list.

Tip #45

Don't Waste a Lot of Time for Little Money

Imagine that you're in your office, the phone rings and it's a company you have been courting for over a year. They finally decide to work with you, but can't pay your fee or buy your products at the current price. What will you do?

Your first option, of course, is to accept the business as a means of establishing a long-term relationship. You can also do your best to negotiate a higher price or flatly reject the offer.

By automatically accepting the lower offer, you send a few messages. One is that of desperation. You may seem too eager to work with them and cause them to question your abilities. On the other hand, you may seem accommodating and willing to do what it takes to please a client. Requesting a higher fee may work to your advantage, especially if you get it. Turning down the business is a serious consideration. If you take the job and despise it, no amount of money will compensate you for your misery. Weighing your options will give you your answer and allow you to justify your decision.

Case in point:

"No" is one word that Bob LeVitus, author of *Dr. Macintosh*, isn't afraid to use. Time is a valuable commodity to him (as it is to many of us), and for him to break away from writing to give a seminar, the amount of money involved needs to justify the amount of time he will need to invest.

He knows what his time is worth and he rarely settles for less. This keeps him focused on what he prefers to do—write. LeVitus enjoys giving presentations, yet when they involve travel, he makes sure that the cost justifies his time away from his family. If not, he is willing to refer the business elsewhere. His family is important to him and he knows not to waste a lot of time for a small amount of money.

Tip #46

Get On Your Clients' Schedule

The part of the country where you do business will often dictate your work schedule. If you live on the West Coast, being an early riser will work to your advantage. If you enjoy sleeping late, you may miss valuable business opportunities.

To meet the demands of your clients, cultivate flexibility as a good quality. Whenever possible, adjust your schedule to meet your clients' needs. Be realistic, however, when setting your hours. Even though you work from home, you shouldn't be expected to answer your phone all night long.

Case in point:

Jane Applegate, syndicated columnist and radio commentator, makes her East Coast calls from 6:30 a.m. to 7:15 a.m., West Coast time. After reaching her East Coast contacts, she takes her kids to school. By 10 a.m. she is back in her office making calls to other parts of the country.

When she is in her new high-tech office, a converted two-car garage that she calls her "corporate headquarters," she spends a majority of her time on the phone. Relocating her office from the middle of her home to the garage has made a big difference in the way she works. She still works around her clients' schedules, but early morning or late-night calls no longer wake up her family.

When she has spent an inordinate amount of time in her home office, she takes a walk long enough to feel refreshed, but not so long that she misses too many calls.

Applegate doesn't mind working around her clients' schedules because this works well with her own schedule. Her method of working gives her a strong balance between her career and her family. She has time to conduct business with her clients and to spend with her family.

Designate one shelf in your bookcase for unread books. It will let you see at a glance what you haven't read and lets you give priority to the books you want to read.

Tip #47
Don't Delegate

It is important to give your staff ample opportunity to make decisions on their own and take responsibility for their actions. Let them contribute to your company through their abilities to handle things that should have been their responsibilities from the beginning.

Business management books often stress the principle of delegation. If you can't do it yourself, give it to someone else. This works in some situations, but not all. A manager who takes responsibility for everything takes equal responsibility when things fail.

Case in point:

"If you take responsibility for something in the first place, it's yours. If you don't, it was never yours to give away," says Scott Gross, of T. Scott Gross and Company, a training, consulting and video production firm. He avoids delegating at all costs because he has complete faith in his staff. He strongly believes that delegating means you had responsibility and gave it away.

Instead of putting himself in a situation where he has to decide who to assign what, he gives each staff person clearly defined job responsibilities. When his office receives a particular request, it automatically goes to the right person.

He expects the people to whom he has given responsibility to make a decision, whether right or wrong. He has little tolerance for indecision. Time is a key factor in his business, and if a staff person agonizes over a decision, it could result in lost income for his company.

Gross welcomes questions and will give advice when asked. His goal is to see his staff succeed and feel good about their decisions. When they make a wrong decision, he discusses it with them, tells them what they did well, what could have been changed and shares a few alternatives.

He realizes that some people may view his attitude about delegation as laziness, yet he would rather be perceived as lazy than a tyrant, unable to abdicate power. This has been a powerful management tool for him and one for which his staff is appreciative.

Tip #48

Develop Strong Follow-Up Techniques

Have you ever had that nagging feeling in the pit of your stomach that you have forgotten to call someone, then followed up only to find out that your competitor has just landed your dream client? Your competitor may not be more qualified for the assignment, yet he or she called at the right time. Your competitor had strong follow-up techniques.

Persistence coupled with a clear follow-up plan definitely pays off. If you call a prospect and he or she asks you to contact the company in a few months, take steps to ensure that you call. If you don't, someone else will.

Make the task of following up easier by using a to-do list, either handwritten or kept electronically. The list will let you know what you need to do and when you need to do it. The list only works if you use it—a bit of common sense that is sometimes ignored. The time to remember that you need to place a call is before, not after, the deadline.

Use a calendar in conjunction with your to-do list. If you have more than one calendar, consolidate the calendars into one. Using more than one to record appointments and deadlines is time-consuming and confusing. You will be more apt to use your calendar if you keep it readily accessible.

If you tell someone that you are going to follow up on a certain day, and even at a certain time, do it. You could lose a sale simply by saying one thing and doing another.

By developing strong follow-up techniques, you will increase your credibility and, more importantly, your opportunity to make more sales and build strong business relationships.

Tip #49
Keep Your Business In Full View

To some, visual reminders, from write on/wipe off boards to wall calendars with important deadlines, are as vital to business as a Teleprompter is to a news anchor. Visuals tell you what to do (or say), and when to do it. If you resort to other types of reminders, for example, a daily planner or desk calendar, you run the risk of dropping the ball on major projects.

In the case of those of you who live your lives by the proverbial "handwriting on the wall," you need to see the big picture and you feel uncomfortable if your visual reminder is not accessible by a mere glance upward. For you, putting everything away could mean the difference between closing the sale or forgetting to follow up.

Case in point:

By keeping his accomplishments and goals in plain sight, Barry Farber, president of Farber Training Systems, Inc., keeps an eye on the past, relishes in the present and plans for the future.

Everything on the walls of his home office has a purpose. The articles about him or written by him, serve to motivate him to future successes. If he has a bad day, he looks to the right of his desk at a wall filled with pho-tographs taken at his many seminars.

The third key item on his wall is a "MAP" (Manage-ment Account Profile), a visual aid designed to help sales managers focus on their teams' activities and to offer a quick overview of how sales reps are managing their territories. (See page 96). The MAP principle is a form of a tickler file system to ensure that you go from the prospect stage to the long-awaited closing.

Farber likes the ability to see, at a glance, what he needs to do and when he needs to do it.

Are you saving money or saving time? Before you rush to save money, evaluate whether your time is worth it.

If you have the choice of making a one- or two-day trip, or staying over a Saturday night to save money, would you be more productive in your home office than in a hotel? The money you save may cost you instead of saving you money.

Is it better to pay someone to do a task for you than for you to do it yourself? Errand-running services are booming because of the lack of time to handle routine tasks.

MANAGEMENT ACCOUNT PROFILE
Sample Eight-Week Analysis

First Call	2nd Stage Presentation	3rd Stage Demo	4th Stage Proposal	5th Stage Close
A	H	J		
B	I			
C				
D				
E				
F				
G				

First Call	2nd Stage Presentation	3rd Stage Demo	4th Stage Proposal	5th Stage Close
A	R	C	H	J	B
E	S	I	F		
K	T	D			
L	U	G			
M					
N					
O					
P					
Q					

WEEK ONE
This is the sales rep's first week of the month in a 30-45 day sales cycle. We see that three accounts have already been moved to the 2nd and 3rd stage of the MAP. The first stage has room for more cards since this is where most of the activity will be generated. In the second week of the sales cycle, the rep still needs to focus on generating new activity in the first stage because most of these accounts will be lost due to competition, unqualified prospect, the prospect stalled, or hopefully, the account moved to the next stage on the MAP. It's crucial to keep a constant flow of activity in each stage, to insure a consistent closing percentage month to month.

WEEK THREE
Additional prospects have been added to the first stage to compensate for the ones who have moved across the board.

First Call	2nd Stage Presentation	3rd Stage Demo	4th Stage Proposal	5th Stage Close

First Call	2nd Stage Presentation	3rd Stage Demo	4th Stage Proposal	5th Stage Close
A	O	C	H	J
B	P	I		
E		D		
F				
G				
K				
L				
M				
N				

WEEK EIGHT
Jumping ahead to week eight, we can now see all the MAP stages filled with activity, representing a highly productive sales rep in action. Note that the first stage should always have twice as many accounts as all the others.

WEEK TWO
Here we see the sales rep has generated six more new accounts in the first stage and moved C,D,H,J accounts across the MAP.

Tip #50

Keep a
'B-Team' List

Why knock yourself out for a limited audience, when others can expose you to a broader group of people? Imagine that while you work with clients, others not affiliated with your business actively promote you to their clients. Without realizing it, you have a built-in network of suppliers, clients and business associates who will be happy to refer you to others. They, in turn, will want you to do the same. It is easier to recommend someone when you feel confident in their abilities and are willing to put your reputation on the line. Unfortunately, a bad referral can reflect poorly on you.

Attempting to market yourself on your own, without the added benefit of others' contacts, is often discouraging and unfulfilling. Being a sole-promoter quickly loses its appeal when you discover that word-of-mouth referral truly is the best form of advertising.

Case in point:

Cross-referring is an invaluable marketing tool for Terri Murphy, speaker, real estate expert and salesperson. She counts on what she calls her B-Team list to promote her to others. The types of people on her list range from interior designers to electricians. She says that she "power-connects" with these people to the benefit of all parties involved. They are familiar with her services and feel comfortable recommending her to the people with whom they work. She feels the same way about them.

When someone on her B Team does a good job, her client is happy, the B Team member is pleased and she is elated.

Are you putting a strain on your memory? Do you remember important tasks, appointments or deadlines when it's too late? Keep your memory from working overtime by relying on more tangible methods.

When you think of something, write it down immediately. If you wait until later, you may have trouble remembering the information.

Keep information you need, including phone numbers, addresses and credit card numbers where you will quickly find them.

Avoid loose scraps of paper and keep appointments and other valuable information in a daily planner, spiral notebook or binder or on your computer. When someone calls you with information, record it in one place to reduce the time spent looking for it.

PERSONAL DEVELOPMENT

Tip #51

Look for Ways to Complement and Supplement Your Skills

Do you know what you don't know? And if so, are you willing to admit it? Unfortunately, some people know what they do well, but refuse to accept that there are areas in which they need help. It may be a matter of a quick phone call or fax, yet they aren't willing to believe that anyone else possesses the skills they lack.

Case in point:

By being brutally honest with herself, Robin Johnson, a partner in Vidalia Associates, a market research and strategic communications consulting firm, realized that she needed help. Six months into her initial business, she carefully weighed her strengths and weaknesses and came to the conclusion that if she was going to succeed, she needed someone to offset her weaknesses.

One weakness was her lack of willingness to market her business. She realized that it was a vital factor to her business, yet she couldn't bring herself to aggressively market her services. She knew that once she secured clients, she would do an outstanding job for them, yet it was her dislike for marketing that held her back.

Her solution? She joined forces with another entrepreneur and Vidalia Associates was formed. Her willingness to acknowledge what needed to be done and to quickly take action paired her with a partner, Meg Fitzpatrick, with whom she has built a solid business. Johnson has skills that her partner lacks and vice versa. They share similar career and personal goals, something that was vital to their agreement to work together.

Johnson, who normally likes to work alone, is still able to do so. Yet when she needs to brainstorm about various projects, her partner is only a phone call or fax away. She doesn't need the personal contact to motivate herself to work, but likes being part of a team.

Johnson has no regrets about starting her first business alone. She felt that it allowed her to test her limits and see how far she could go on her own.

Tip #52

Live What You Teach

Some people do what they say they'll do, while others say one thing and do another. Living by example is a key to success. It is difficult to believe someone when their actions do not correspond with what they say.

If your business helps others improve their communications skills, you need to be an effective communicator. That's common sense, yet it is so common, you may forget it.

Knowing that others look to you for advice and guidance makes it imperative that you think about what you say before you say it, and if you say you are going to do it, do it.

Case in point:

What happens when a tightwad shares her ideas with others, for a price, and her income skyrockets to six figures? She keeps living the same as she did before. Amy Dacyczyn, publisher and author of *The Tightwad Gazette,* lives the lifestyle she teaches. She shares information with her readers about how to get more for their money.

From her home office in Leeds, Maine, she writes and publishes a monthly newsletter for diehard tightwads. Her subscriber base continues to grow through word of mouth and national television appearances.

When her income reached a substantial six-figures from the newsletter and her book, friends wondered if she would abandon the frugal lifestyle and pay retail. She said, "No way," and continues to scrimp and save. She and her husband have established college funds for their six children and have invested in rental property.

The rapid growth of her business has precipitated the need to hire staff. She is learning to delegate more and keeps her eye on the bottom line.

Dacyczyn could have given in to the allure of money, yet she knows that that is against her beliefs. She says that her business is not about making money, but about believing in what you do.

Tip #53

When It's No Longer Fun, Quit

Some people work for a living, while others play. Don't be surprised if those playing are more successful than those working. Successful home office professionals attribute much of their success to doing what they enjoy. It is common sense to do what you love. Do you love what you do?

Punching an imaginary time clock, doing time and meeting the needs of others is not how many want to spend their lives, yet they do. Their job is a means to an end—their paycheck. Successful home office professionals see work differently. Their jobs, or what some call their hobbies, are the *reward*. The money they earn is the icing on the cake.

Many of them say that if they were not paid to do their work, they wouldn't mind. Of course, in reality, lack of payment might increase their willingness to accept money. Here's the point: They enjoy what they do. When they are in their offices, or working with clients, that's where they want to be.

Some people say that they have made pacts with themselves: When their professions or businesses are no longer fun, they will quit and do something else. This may be as simple as phasing out a division of their company, or discontinuing a product or service that no longer benefits them or is not worth the frustration it causes.

Home office professionals need only travel a busy highway during rush hour and view zombie-like drivers to affirm their belief that the choice they made to work at home is the right one. These people know that if what they have chosen is wrong, they can start another business.

Is there a missing link between the scheduling program on your computer and your paper-based planner? Print your schedule and to-do list on pre-cut sheets that fit in your daily planner. This will eliminate the need for hand-written information from one source to the other.

Tip #54

Schedule 'Brag Time' Each Day

What do comedians, singers and professional speakers have in common? They receive applause and sometimes a standing ovation for a job well-done. Unfortunately, in the business world, very few people receive even a pat on the back when they perform well. They may receive a bonus or a raise, but the physical outpouring of support is often lacking.

At the end of each day, take a close look at your schedule, or to do list, and review what you have accomplished. Ask yourself what went well for you, and what things happened that should make you proud. Then tell someone.

Case in point:

Making others feel good is part of Joe Charbonneau's job. As the president of Presentations, Inc., he travels around the country training and motivating others. He practices what he preaches, and encourages his staff to hold "brag time" at the end of each day.

When Charbonneau arrives in town, he assembles his staff and they each share their accomplishments for the day. He encourages his staff to brag about the things they did, no matter how small.

On the days when Charbonneau is out of town, the brag-time tradition continues. Instead of bragging in person, staff members leave brag-time messages on his voice mail. They list all of the people they contacted by phone and how many presentations they closed.

Brag time lets Charbonneau's staff know that he cares about their accomplishments and that they deserve their own personal standing ovation.

Tip #55

Create Your Own
Unique Identity

It is easy to copy what someone else is doing, modify it a bit and present it as your own. That may work for a while, but eventually you will run out of material, lose your identity and you will need to search for another specialty.

Bob Vila is known for home improvement, while Martha Stewart reigns as the queen of entertaining. What are you known for? When people discuss a topic with which you are familiar, do they think of you or someone else?

The old saying, "Jack of all trades, master of none" can come painfully true. If others perceive you as being able to do everything, they will ignore those things that you do better than others. Those special skills will get lost in the clutter of the other skills you are eager to share.

Case in point:

Doing what everyone else does would have kept Scott Gross, a professional speaker and author, close to home. He knows that if his seminars and keynotes offer nothing different from anyone else's, people can get the same information from a junior college.

Gross went on a mission to discover his own identity. He focused on what he did well, and determined he worked well with customers. He knew how to make customers happy and bring them back for more. That is when he developed his "Positively Outrageous Service" (POS). Since then he has shared his message to audiences around the country.

Gross knew that it would be time-consuming to develop his own theories about how customers want to be treated. He also knew that he didn't want to be just another customer-service speaker. He set a goal to be different.

Tip #56

Get Support From the People at Home

If you worked in a corporate office before opening your home office, you probably considered your home a respite from the storm of business life. If you didn't like your boss, you could feel comfort in knowing that your loving family awaited you at home. What happens when you move your office home?

When your office situation changes, you will spend more time at home, making it crucial that your family supports your efforts.

Any stress that your family directs toward you will ultimately affect your work productivity. Instead of pushing them away, think of ways to include them in your business by discussing problems with them, asking their opinion or, more importantly, sharing your successes with them.

If your family members feel left out of your business, they will soon learn to resent your work and any time you spend in your home office. They don't have to be involved to the point of making phone calls for you or taking messages. Instead, use them as a sounding board, or a means of developing new ideas. Someone not so closely tied to your business or industry may provide you with ideas that had never occurred to you.

Tip #57

Take Joy Breaks

The words "work" and "fun" are rarely spoken in the same breath. Common business practice tells you that to be productive, you must be relentless and keep pushing yourself until you finish. You may feel that the harder you work, the more productive you become. The opposite is true. The more you push yourself, the less effective you will be. Fatigue will set in and much of the work you accomplish will have to be redone.

Instead of working to the point of exhaustion, stop what you are doing and take a break. When you return to your desk, you will feel refreshed and will often discover answers to questions over which you had agonized for hours. Your demands as a home office professional are unending. Your weapon against boredom, repetition and fatigue is to take breaks and, most of all, give yourself a break.

Case in point:

Dr. Ann McGee-Cooper, author of *You Don't Have to Go Home From Work Exhausted*, coined the phrase "joy breaks," to describe time not spent working, but playing. She fills her home office with toys, games, puzzles and stuffed animals, ready to be enjoyed throughout the day.

McGee-Cooper encourages her "inner-child" to come out whenever it wants to play. She knows that taking life seriously and gliding through the rough waters of business is more fun when you let go and laugh.

Joy breaks not only serve to get you away from what you are doing, but they actually re-energize you and make it easier for you to get back to work. Playing may seem awkward and unbusiness-like at first, yet breaks may become a vital part of your workday.

Tip #58

Don't Be Afraid to Be Alone

Working within a home office can be lonely. For some people, this is an ideal situation, while others need personal contact. They may find themselves looking forward to the UPS man's delivery. Although the home office worker may be on the phone with clients, it is not the same as face-to-face meetings and personal interactions.

Ease the loneliness, while enhancing your business, by setting up meetings with other home office professionals. You could meet on a designated day each week and discuss marketing ideas, promotional plans and anything else to improve the way you do business. Sometimes having a set place to go will give you the motivation to work alone.

Anyone who has gone from an outside corporate office to a home office, and has had to endure countless interruptions from associates, can appreciate the value of being alone. The sheer reduction in interruptions often ensures a higher quality of work in less time.

Case in point:

When he started his business, Gene Busnar, collaborative writer and author of numerous books, found that being with others in an outside office was important to him. He soon realized, however, that the long commute he made to his office represented a "useless experience," and he moved his business to his home.

Although Busnar works alone in his home office, he makes an effort to leave his office each day and be around others, whether he schedules a lunch with a colleague or attends an organization meeting. He has adjusted to being alone, supplementing his work style with outside contact, and knows that he is now more productive.

Tip #59

You Have to Fail Before You Can Succeed

No one likes to fail or makes plans to do so, yet failure is a part of business. Most of us fear failure, but the wise professional can see failure as an opportunity.

There is always something good that can be culled from failure. You just have to look for it.

Products from Post-it™ notes to Silly Putty™ were deemed "failures" at the beginning. Yet, as they say, the rest is history. Before you write off a failure and take great pains to conceal your mistakes, spend time learning from what you have done. See your failure from a different point of view, and you will open your mind to new opportunities and future successes.

When you feel overwhelmed by the mistakes you make, or have trouble discovering the good part of a bad situation, start a "What I Learned" journal. It may sound corny, but making yourself record the lesson you learned from a mistake takes the worry off your mind.

Let's say you spent more than you could afford on a direct-mail campaign, convinced that you couldn't fail. Three weeks later, instead of orders pouring into your office, bills for printing are filling your mailbox. All that you have to show for your time, money and effort are expenses. What's the lesson? Buy a better mailing list or avoid direct mail. Recording the lesson lets you see in black and white that there was a good part to your mistake after all.

After you record your mistake, you no longer have to dwell on it or, as some people do, obsess over it. Worrying about what you have done or have forgotten to do will not change the end result. It can, however, change the way you handle the same situation in the future.

Failure doesn't have to be seen as negative. After all, without failure, success wouldn't be so sweet.

Tip #60

Treat Yourself as a Client and Take Care of Yourself

When it comes to your clients, there is often little you will not do to meet their needs. Yet your zeal to please your clients may cause you to forget your own needs. Ignoring your health, family and personal time seems to be a small sacrifice at first. After a while, you may grow to resent what you have sacrificed for the sake of your business.

Case in point:

By following a simple yet practical rule, John Osborne, of Osborne Applegate, attends to his needs and keeps his excitement for his business high. His thriving consulting business takes him around the country, and away from other activities, including exercise. Rather than wait for the perfect time to work out, he schedules exercise on his calendar and treats it the way he would an appointment with a client.

Pacing himself is important, too. He realizes his limitations and stops working when he has accomplished the goals he has set for the day. He enjoys his business, yet realizes that too much of a good thing can be harmful and ultimately lead to burnout.

Keeping up with the changes in his industry means mounds of magazines that he must read. He schedules uninterrupted reading time to plow through the magazines to uncover the information he needs.

When he schedules time for himself, he also includes time for his family. He gives his clients "world-class service," and treats himself with the same respect.

Tip #61

Big Egos Miss Big Opportunities

Public figures are often warned against believing their own positive press, and to avoid becoming *prima donnas*. The same advice holds true in business. The more articles about you or by you, the more compliments you will undoubtedly receive, and the more you may start believing everything others say.

There is nothing wrong with a strong sense of self-esteem. When you are confident, you tend to bring that confidence out in others. There is something wrong, however, with an ego so large that it leaves little room for others.

Case in point:

After reading his byline in various national magazines, and profiles of his business and accomplishments in other publications, Barry Farber could have easily let his ego run his business. When a client or prospect called, he could have treated them as if he were doing them a favor to talk with them, instead of searching for ways to meet their needs. Farber has chosen the latter method.

As the author of *State of the Art Selling*, an audiotape program and book, Farber feels confident in his abilities to help his clients meet their needs, yet is realistic enough to know that if he alienates clients, they will turn to someone else. He has seen colleagues turn away business that they felt was beneath them, only to learn that the clients they turned away turned into major accounts...for someone else. They let their ego guide them straight to a dead end.

Farber often questions himself about what he can do differently. He knows that anyone who is interested in succeeding needs to learn constantly. Believing that he doesn't know everything, he strives to be well-rounded in all areas.

PERSONAL
WORK HABITS

Tip #62
Don't Be Afraid to Change What Isn't Working

Determination can be an admirable quality. In some cases, it is crucial for achieving success. In some individuals, it can prevent success. It's valuable to know when your determination gets in the way of fulfilling your goals and desires. Change is difficult for many. It conjures up a wide range of emotions, from fear of the unknown to fear of failure. There is a sense of calm that accompanies the same routine, while change upsets the balance and takes you out of your comfort zone. Change doesn't have to be that way.

Don't attempt to change everything at once. That can be terrifying and intimidating. Instead, make changes little by little and, when you feel more comfortable, move on to something else. When you face your feelings about change, you will more readily accept it, and even welcome it.

Case in point:

Change is a good friend to Joe Charbonneau, a nationally known professional speaker and president of Presentations, Inc. He acknowledges that doing the same thing all of the time leads to failure. Charbonneau makes it a point to constantly monitor what he and his staff do, and if something is not working, he changes it.

Charbonneau's staff used to handle all printing jobs (especially large ones) in-house. They also took care of dubbing his audio tapes. Charbonneau finally realized that what at first appeared to be a good idea was neither cost-effective nor time-efficient. Now all duplication is handled by other companies.

Charbonneau knows that it is not easy to admit that you have made an error in judgment, or have implemented an idea that looked better on paper than in action. However, refusing to make a change means a willingness to accept the consequences of stubbornness. The person who can face the fact that there is a better way will be rewarded with endless opportunities.

Tip #63

Don't Be Afraid to Charge What You're Worth

Changing your fee structure is an inevitable part of any business. How you handle the change and when you choose to increase your rates may determine if you maintain your same income or break through to a new level. A client who has been with you since the beginning is hard to relinquish. Yet, if the services you provide far exceed what you charge, you may soon resent your working relationship.

There are a few options. You can maintain your fee structure, gradually increase your fees and offer more services each time, or raise your fees and risk losing your client.

Case in point:

Change is a large part of Terry Brock's business as a professional speaker who teaches individuals and businesses how to use computers and technology. As the computer industry experiences more changes (somewhat daily), Brock's expertise increases in value each year.

As his business grew and demand for his expertise skyrocketed, he had to make a choice. Should he maintain his client base, his fees and turn down new clients who would pay more? He enjoyed working with his current clients and gradually raised his fees with those who could afford it and gave up those who could not. They parted on good terms and he left the door open for further opportunities with these companies. When the former clients have larger budgets, they are able to bring Brock back to their company.

Brock now works with larger companies and has expanded the services he offers. In addition to speaking, he offers audio and videotapes that his clients can review to reinforce his message. It was difficult to let go of his old clients, yet he knew that the separation served everyone's best interest.

Tip #64

Get Dressed for Work

Until the video phone becomes more affordable and prominent, home office professionals are safe from the office "fashion police." Even though many outside offices have dispensed with a dress code and home office professionals are not required to follow one, some professionals still adhere to a standard of appearance even though they work in their own homes.

A few home office professionals feel that they can't truly be professional unless they put on a suit and tie, or a dress and heels. For some it is habit, especially if they have worked in an outside office for years. These people tie their professionalism to their appearance, even though they may be the only ones who see themselves dressed this way.

On days when you feel less confident or lack the motivation to work, put on your business suit and get to work—or at least shed your bathrobe and put on presentable jeans and a shirt. It may just give you the psychological boost you need.

Case in point:

Regardless of whether she has an appointment with a client, Lynn Armstrong, owner of an advertising specialty company, dresses for work each day. Each day she imagines that she is going to see her best client and dresses accordingly.

Armstrong's strict dress code keeps her from getting distracted. If she dresses in professional attire, she believes she will refrain from doing a load of laundry or washing dishes. She focuses on her work and spends the day on work-related tasks.

She feels that dressing up for work makes her more productive. In addition, when she dresses for work, she can quickly join her friends for lunch without wasting time changing into something more appropriate.

Tip #65

Keep Yourself On Track

A boss looming over your shoulder, watching your next move, is often enough incentive to make anyone keep writing, selling or marketing, whether you want to or not. What happens when you're the only one in your office and the only thing looming over you is a deadline? What keeps you from turning off your computer and turning on your television? Discipline.

One of the advantages of working from home is the flexibility it affords and the absence of co-workers or a boss in your office. With freedom, however, comes responsibility. Obviously, if you don't work, your productivity and, eventually, your income will suffer.

There's a happy medium. On the days when you feel more inclined to write a letter to a friend rather than a report for a client, find ways to motivate yourself to work.

Start by convincing yourself to work for 30 minutes or an hour. Don't be surprised to find yourself working longer than you anticipated. Working on a project is usually the easy part. Getting started is more difficult. The more you postpone a project, the heavier it weighs in the back of your mind.

Another method to improve your discipline is to set a small goal, for example sending two letters to prospects. When you reach that goal, reward yourself. You can watch television for 15 minutes or read your favorite magazine. Whatever the reward, make it meaningful and worth obtaining.

Discipline means different things to different people. You can always change your level of discipline, whereas the time you waste can never be replaced.

Tip #66

Don't Give
Your Ideas Away

Maintaining a professional yet profitable business means that you need to handle occasional requests for advice carefully. If you spend an inordinate amount of time on the phone offering free advice, you may be inadvertently encouraging future calls that will take away from your time—and income. The key is to create a balance between what advice and time you are willing to give away and how you will be compensated for your time.

Case in point:

By implementing a program whereby clients can work with him over the phone, public relations counselor Alan Caruba has solved the problem of callers soliciting free advice. Through his "PR Hotline," Caruba provides public relations advice at an hourly rate of $100. With his services in demand and his time limited, his phone consultation service is a viable alternative to clients. Otherwise, they would have to pay Caruba for travel time and expenses.

Caruba starts by scheduling a one-hour consultation, and requests in advance material about the caller's company. He evaluates the information before their call and is ready to offer suggestions during their phone meeting. The preparation he does in advance helps him to identify his client's problems and provide solutions. He knows that a few callers just "want the facts" while others will need future phone consultations.

Caruba no longer feels uncomfortable when someone calls asking for advice. He tells them about the PR Hotline and if they are interested, he schedules an appointment on the spot.

Caruba knows the value of his time and expertise and is not afraid to put a price on it.

Tip #67

Charities: Donate Time or Talent Instead of Money

If you receive a request from a charity, a homeless shelter for example, don't feel that because you're short on cash, you can't help out. Take your mind off money and focus your talents.

Another option is merchandise. Although something may be of minimal cost to you, the charity could sell your donation during an auction or garage sale. Think creatively and give what you feel comfortable donating, whether it's your time, talent, service or product.

Some people see charity events as a way to promote their businesses and secure tax write-offs. That's the wrong attitude and approach. Self-promoters' intentions are rarely kept to themselves. Eventually, the charity and the public become acutely aware of this strategy. Don't be surprised, however, if your charitable contribution comes back to you in the form of business or new contracts.

Case in point:

By donating her talent for creating unusual and memorable designs, Diana Craft, a designer and illustrator, has helped various charities save money and make money. Her time to volunteer at a charity is limited, so instead, she donates her talent. A brochure, flier or logo may take only a few hours of her time to design, yet saves the charity hundreds of dollars on agency design costs. She enjoys helping others by doing something she loves to do anyway.

Tip #68

Don't Be Left Out In a Corporate Turnover

In the revolving door of the corporate world, people spin in and out of jobs. Some leave by choice, while others are discreetly removed from their positions. One day you may be dealing with the president of the company, and the next day discover a new nameplate on his or her door.

When your old contact is replaced with another, will you be kept in the loop and maintain the client or be thrown for a loop?

Case in point:

Terry Brock, president of Achievement Systems, Inc., and a professional speaker, acutely aware that at any moment his corporate contacts may change, keeps in touch with them on a regular basis. He speaks with his clients via long distance to keep abreast of new developments. When he is in town, he schedules face-to-face meetings with his contacts and those who work closely with his contacts.

Because most of his business is repeat business, Brock is known for building strong relationships with his clients. Often when someone he's worked with at one company leaves to work for another, he is hired by that individual to work with the new company. In these situations, his former clients are already familiar with the quality of his work, enabling him to start working with them again immediately.

Brock realizes that there will always be a fresh supply of new people to replace his old contacts. He no longer dreads those changes since he has already laid the groundwork for a new relationship and is able to make the transition a smooth one.

PUBLIC RELATIONS

Tip #69
Establish Yourself as an Expert

Physicians, attorneys and law enforcement officials, among others, are considered experts in their fields because they must pass a series of tests to receive their degrees or certification. If you're outside these fields, establishing yourself as an expert will take innovative thinking.

When someone has a problem or the press wants a quote from an expert, how do you get them to call you first? There are several ways.

First, write articles for various publications that cater to your profession. By appearing often in trade publications, you will soon become a household name within your profession.

Teach courses in your field (see Tip #32). When someone is looking for an expert, your credentials as an instructor will lend credibility to your talents.

Make yourself available to the media by sending or faxing press releases concerning your area of interest. Offer tips to help a publication's readers or a station's listeners.

Case in point:

Quite by accident, Amy Dacyczyn, publisher of "The Tightwad Gazette," became an expert. When she started publishing her newsletter, she didn't feel that she was an expert. She merely wanted to share with others what worked for her.

As her newsletter became more popular, the media began to take notice and ask her to share her tightwad secrets. They even filmed segments in her home, to show how she lived a tightwad lifestyle.

In addition to being quoted in articles, she started writing articles for newspapers and national magazines. Her first book, *The Tightwad Gazette*, a compilation of her past newsletters, further established her as the expert in saving money.

Tip #70

Don't Play
Hide and Seek

Imagine that your phone rings and it's the producer of a national morning television show, asking you to be a guest on the program. Another call may come from a writer from a national publication, asking for an interview.

For some, this is a common occurrence. Others only dream of the day when they will see their names and faces on television or in print. You may have prepared for the big day when you "go national" or even regional, practiced what you will say and even know what you will wear, yet you may have forgotten to include one thing—your city.

With publicity, it is unrealistic to think that a television program or publication will include your address and phone number. On rare occasions, it will, but don't count on it.

There's still hope, however. Whenever you're quoted, include your name, title and city. For example, a computer expert might identify himself as John Doe, Alaska-based computer expert. If he chooses to use his company name instead of his city, viewers or readers will have no idea how to reach him.

Don't count on the station or the publication to provide callers with your name and phone number. They keep busy schedules and may not want to serve as your secretary after your appearance airs or article runs. Whenever possible, opt for mentioning your city over your company name.

Mentioning your city is important, but you need to be listed in the telephone directory as well. If you mention your city and callers are unable to find your number in the business listings, the publicity will not immediately benefit you. It is a good idea to have at least one business line, instead of operating your business using your personal line.

Publicity is an ideal way to increase your exposure and, ultimately, your sales. Make it easy for people to find you.

Tip #71

Have a One-Page Fact Sheet Available

When reporters call—and if you're actively promoting yourself they will—will you be able to provide them with information about your company? You may have a brochure, yet the brochure may be filled with too much information to read at a glance. Besides, four-color brochures don't always fax clearly.

Case in point:

When a reporter calls Alan Caruba, public relations counselor, editorial consultant and lecturer, he has a one page, up-to-date and accurate "fact sheet" ready to fax.

He uses the sheet as a pre-interview piece, to give the reporter a feel for his background and expertise, or as a post-interview piece to provide the reporter with additional information. Caruba always offers to send the sheet, even if the reporter hasn't requested it.

Caruba stresses that the one-page sheet should be designed and printed to make it readable by fax. If you create an elaborate sheet that faxes poorly, it is of little benefit to you. Caruba recommends including information ranging from your company's history, to what you are selling or doing. Also include your credentials.

A one-page fact sheet is also the ideal accompaniment to a news release. In that the release will be about a timely event or new product or service, you will be limited in the amount of information you can include about your company. The fact sheet will provide additional insight, without taking away from the release.

Tip #72

Advertise
Through Action

Action speaks louder than words. You can tell someone something, yet if you show them, they are more apt to remember. If you handle a situation outside of a business setting, for example, volunteer at the school carnival, or chair the fund-raising committee for a community service group, the level of professionalism you exhibit will reflect favorably on your business.

Unavoidably, you are a walking advertisement for your business. If you are president of the PTA or a den leader, your talents and professionalism may be called into question. How you handle situations not directly associated with your business can change others' perception of you and what you are capable of doing.

Case in point:

A willingness to do more than is expected keeps Dorothy Collins, president of Organization Administrators, Inc., in demand. Whether she is handling the minute details of a client's annual convention or donating her time to the various business groups to which she belongs, she is advertising herself.

She has demonstrated her penchant for details while orchestrating the conventions of her clients and earned the business of the attendees who belong to other associations. They see what she can do for one association and want their association to receive the same treatment and attention to details.

Collins knows that the way she handles something on a volunteer basis reflects the manner in which she manages her day-to-day business. No amount of sales information or flashy brochures have convinced her clients of her outstanding abilities to manage their associations as much as her proven abilities.

Is your newsletter pile overflowing?

Designate a reading spot for incoming newsletters and other reading material. When you receive a newsletter, immediately put it in there until you are ready to read it.

If the newsletter is short, scan it when it comes in if you have a few minutes to spare. Highlight the points that you will refer to later.

Store newsletters that you use as resources, in file folders or notebooks labeled with the name of the newsletters.

Tip #73

Produce a
Tips Booklet

You may have toyed with the idea of gathering your ideas, organizing them and compiling them into a book to sell nationwide. That's a reasonable goal, yet it requires time, dedication and, in some cases, money. Rather than dedicate yourself to this lofty goal, think smaller and compress your ideas into a booklet.

Case in point:

When Alan Caruba, public relations counselor, editorial consultant and editor of *Power Media Selects*, distributes a news release, the media take notice. Within the release, not only does he provide valuable information sent to the right person, but he regularly offers tips booklets for sale, to give the reader additional information about the topic.

One of his booklets, "Don't Panic! An Instant Guide to Crisis Communications," grew out of a checklist for crisis control that he offered at no charge to the readers of a public relations trade newsletter. The overwhelming response from readers convinced him to publish this booklet that sells for $5.

Another booklet he created, "Beating Boredom: Ten Secrets To Avoid Boredom," is published under the umbrella of his company, The Caruba Organization. He offers the booklet as part of his "Boring Institute," an internationally famed media spoof and clearinghouse of information on boredom. When he distributes a news release about the Boring Institute's list of "The Most Boring Celebrities of the Year" or "The Most Boring Films of the Year Awards," he mentions the booklet.

In his news releases and during interviews, he makes it a point to include his address, but not his phone number—he fields enough calls already—plus the cost of the booklet. Offering the booklet entices readers to contact him, and the cost more than covers his printing expenses.

THE CARUBA ORGANIZATION

Box 40, Maplewood, NJ 07040
[Office] 201/763-6392 • [Facsimile] 201/763-4287

AT LAST . . .
AN EASY, HAND-HELD GUIDE THAT TELLS YOU WHAT TO DO WHEN A CRISIS EVENT OCCURS

✓ Written by Alan Caruba, a veteran PR Counselor to corporations, associations, professionals, and entrepreneurs from coast to coast.

✓ Provides the ten top trade secrets of effective crisis communications control procedures.

✓ Opens up into a poster/checklist with nearly 50 options to activate, depending on the scope of the crisis event.

✓ Priced at only **$5.00** per copy.

✓ And, if you act now, you can receive the unique bonus of **free PR counseling!**

Excerpt from Michael Levine's book, *Guerrilla P.R.*: "Although he's one of the most in-demand public relations counselors and counts major associations, corporations, and celebrities among his clients, Alan Caruba of Maplewood, NJ, possesses the soul of a Guerrilla P.R. master."

A December 1993 *Washington Post* profile described Alan Caruba as a public relations professional who knows how to achieve "unnerving quantities of air time and column inches."

"There's a virtual state of siege in America regarding every kind of agricultural, industrial, institutional, professional and other business activity," says Caruba. "**This guide is designed to help everyone** instantly grasp what to do and how to do it when any kind of crisis event occurs, attracting potentially damaging media coverage."

Reprinted with permission from The Caruba Organization

Tip #74

Advertising Doesn't Always Pay

You may have heard the saying, "Advertising doesn't cost, it pays." For some businesses, advertising is essential, while others would be better off donating their advertising budget to charity.

Case in point:

When interior designer Sharon Sistine opened her design firm, she contemplated whether she should advertise. She knew the type of clientele she had in mind, yet wasn't sure they would respond to paid advertisements. She opted to go for word-of-mouth referrals.

At one point, she was so busy, she converted her number to an unlisted one. Clients still called her. By keeping a low profile, she had more work than she could handle, and was able to pick and choose her clients.

The interior design business has changed since Sistine entered it 25 years ago. It is more competitive, and as the economy stays on a roller coaster, some who considered interior design a necessity now consider it a luxury. Sistine's client base continues to grow, however, without paid advertising.

Instead of advertising, Sistine relies on publicity to spread the word about her business. Multi-page spreads featuring her work have been published in various magazines, including *House and Garden.*

Sistine realizes that advertising is the perfect avenue for some. But for her type of business, she believes that "good work gets work." And when people see her work, they're sold.

Tip #75

Tell Your Clients About Your Achievements—Often

What happens when you have something nice to say about yourself? Do you allow yourself to say it or do you let your modesty get in the way?

No one can promote *you* better than you, and since actions speak louder than words, be willing to share your accomplishments with others, especially your clients. When you do have something positive to say, put that air to use and blow your own horn.

Case in point:

As an internationally known photojournalist, Art Shay knows that modesty and shyness present two barriers on the road to success. Shay has a wealth of knowledge gained over the past 44 years, through shooting thousands of covers for national magazines, including *Time* and *Life*. When talking with prospects or clients, he shares his experiences.

Shay has a way of mentioning his accomplishments that is both disarming and unassuming. He knows that good public relations means more business. If a client is aware of what he has done and can do, the client will hire him to do more.

Shay doesn't limit his broadcasting of achievements to himself. He happily promotes his wife's rare-books bookstore or his children's' photography businesses. When he believes in what someone is doing, he wants others to know about it.

He sends his clients articles he has authored, and the tearsheets from publications in which his photographs have been published. He wants clients to be up-to-date on his activities, and to think of him for their next assignment.

Tip #76

Choose Fax Over Mail When It Comes to Media

The US Postal Service is somewhat archaic compared to overnight mail, faxing and transmitting information via modem. The slogan, "When you have to get it there overnight," could be changed to, "When you have to get it there in three minutes or less." When dealing with the media, there is a right and wrong way to disseminate information.

Case in point:

In the media game, where it's hit or miss whether your news release will be picked up, Alan Caruba, a seasoned public relations counselor, is often a winner. As technology has changed, so has Caruba's approach to staying in contact with the media.

Since his releases are timely, Caruba regularly faxes them to his media contacts. He says that faxing should be limited to newsworthy stories that are tied to some event happening within the next 48 hours. Caruba also recommends faxing information as a follow-up to a telephone interview.

Not all releases or information, however, should be faxed. Caruba cites the example of a national association with a press kit filled with information. Instead of faxing page after page, the organization should send the information instead. If they are contacting the media about a specific event, they could fax a news release, along with a one-page fact sheet (see Tip #71) then send the press kit if the reporter needs additional information.

Caruba stresses that a fax sent to the wrong editor is a waste of your time and their fax paper. Editors are inundated with information, and if you fax it to the wrong person, by the time it reaches the right person (if it's passed on), it may be too late.

RESEARCH

Tip #77

Read What You Need

Our society, filled with interactive television, 24-hour-a-day news broadcasts and talk shows covering everything we ever wanted to know (or didn't want to know, for that matter) about everything, has spawned a new breed of information maniacs.

We want to know everything and know it *now*. As newspapers roll off the presses, a new story breaks. By the time we get the next day's edition, we have heard the story from every point of view on every TV station.

At some point you have to say "enough!" There are only 24 hours in each day and only so much information that you can process during that time. Limit your reading to what you need to know. At first, you may feel discouraged that you don't know the minute details of a peace accord or why the stock market tumbles and leaps. At the same time, you will have information pertinent to your life.

Case in point:

Dr. Ann McGee-Cooper, a consultant and the author of *You Don't Have To Go Home From Work Exhausted* and *Time Management For Unmanageable People*, equates books with people. She recommends reading a book like a person by reading the parts you want to know about and forgetting about the sections that are not as pertinent. She reads two books each week, in addition to numerous magazines. These books and magazines cover 38 fields of interest to her.

Rather than read every word, she skims certain chapters while focusing intently on others. When someone she knows reads the same book, that person may point out a section she missed. At that point she will read that section to obtain the information she needs. She is able to read more books and cover more material because she reads selectively.

Tip #78
Seek Information From Nontraditional Sources

Business clubs and associations offer a way to test ideas and brainstorm with others. Some groups are exclusive to your profession, while others encourage a mix of business owners to provide balance. If you are unsatisfied with the amount and level of resources available to you locally, additional help is only a phone call away.

Case in point:

Publishing a catalog for executive recruiters was a project that Bill Vick, owner of three businesses, including Vick & Associates, an executive search firm, spent months researching. He talked to others in the executive search field to ask their opinions, yet felt that something was missing.

Instead of merely relying on the advice he had gathered from his colleagues, Vick utilized electronics and went on-line, searching for additional information. He posted the following message on CompuServe, "I'm starting a catalog business and need business help, advice and guidance." Several people responded to his request and two included phone numbers. He called both of them and gained valuable insight into the catalog business. One of those who responded gave Vick advice that he had never considered. Vick knows that at least one of the ideas he garnered will save him money and aggravation.

By calling upon nontraditional resources available to him, Vick gained insight into the catalog business and shaved months off of his learning curve. With the touch of a few buttons, he has access to professionals in several fields other than his own.

Tip #79
Ask 'So What?'

When you run your business the same way, day after day, it is easy to get so caught up in what you do that you become complacent. You no longer strive for something different or better, and feel comfortable with your current status.

The thought of a new idea may be mentally draining and hardly seem worth the effort. Doing the same thing is easier and safer. Take the time to challenge yourself, leave your comfort zone and stretch your imagination. The results can be unlimited. You will open yourself to new opportunities that you otherwise may have overlooked.

Case in point:

Looking for things to fix, even when they may not be broken, keeps Scott Gross on his toes. As the creator of Positively Outrageous Service in both seminar and book form, he never feels satisfied with what he is currently doing and searches for ways to do everything better. Gross always knows that another great idea is just around the bend.

To test his ideas and those of others, he implements the "So what?" test. This determines if an idea he or one of his staff has, has merit. If after hearing an idea or presenting a new concept, he says or hears, "So what?"

the idea goes back to the old drawing board. Gross does not believe in change for the sake of change.

Gross encourages his staff to take the "So what?" test before they present anything to him. He knows that they are capable of innovative ideas and may need a reminder that a great idea is always around the bend.

He never knows when a new idea will pop into his head. Yet, when it does, he is always ready to test it.

Tip #80
See What Your Competition Is Doing and Change Your Approach

Competition brings out the best in some people and the worst in others. Some welcome the added pressure and the opportunity to prove that they offer the best service or product.

Research your competition honestly. Never mislead competitors by posing as a large client to obtain its marketing and pricing information. Call competitors directly and ask for it. You may be surprised at their willingness to share information. Still, be persistent, and after awhile you will find someone willing to talk with you. That person will undoubtedly be aware that in most industries, there is room for everyone.

If you speak with individuals out of state, thereby lessening the chances that you will compete directly, be willing to pay for their time. They may not accept your offer, yet you are saying to them that their time is valuable and you are willing to pay for it.

When you call competitors, tell them about your business and stress that you are going to make your business different. You may become the person to whom this competitor refers business. Unbeknownst to you, you may be entering a field that the competitor has relinquished or has been considering discontinuing.

Talk to people who are using a competitor's services and find out what's missing. Determine if there is some aspect of that business that, if added, would enhance the product or service. As consumers, potential clients will have a different view of your industry than you.

Take the time to research how to make your business different from someone else's. You will have a greater chance of succeeding and maintaining a working relationship with clients.

When asking others for advice and guidance, be prepared and considerate of their time.

Make your first request in writing. Keep it to one page and clearly state your questions. If you do not receive a request after one month, follow up with a phone call.

If you prefer to call, ask the individual if he or she has 10 minutes to talk and don't exceed that 10 minutes.

Another option is to schedule a phone appointment. That will give the person you are calling time to prepare some answers. If you are calling long distance, call at your expense.

Tip #81

Be Prepared for Sudden Growth

Even the most detailed business plan may not prepare you for a sudden burst of business. Initially, you may enjoy the commotion it can cause, but eventually you will face a common dilemma—too much work and not enough help.

The simple solution would be to do what the big corporations do and hire a staff or increase your present one. This involves hiring and training time, which most businesses cannot afford to lose. If you plan ahead, you can save time and money when the demand for your product or service exceeds your supply.

Case in point:

Through a conscientious effort to market their business, Robin Johnson and Meg Fitzpatrick, partners in Vidalia Associates, a market research firm, exceeded the number of clients they projected to obtain. They had underestimated how quickly they could grow and had more work than they could handle.

You may find it difficult to feel sorry for them. After all, who wouldn't want that problem?

They were grateful for the business, while at the same time, frustrated. Their frustration stemmed from a lack of foresight. They felt confident that their business would eventually succeed, yet their definition of eventually and what actually happened varied by at least one year.

Their solution has been to hire subcontractors to handle the overflow, including data processing work.

Johnson is pleased with her subcontractors, yet makes it a point to monitor their progress and quality of work on a regular basis. Anything they do could reflect poorly on her business and damage the relationships she and her partner have worked so hard to develop. They have earned a strong reputation in their industry and are careful to nurture that reputation.

SALES

Tip #82
Look Past Your Clients' Business Lives

It is easy to see a client as one-dimensional. It is important to remember that your clients have lives outside of the corporate world. They have families, belong to various organizations, and are in contact with people you will never meet face-to-face. They offer opportunities for you to increase your business if you search for them.

When meeting with a client in person, take a close look at his or her office. Does the client have photographs of children in sports uniforms? Are there plaques on the wall to award the client's coaching efforts? Be alert to these hints of another life and you will see ways to be of further service to your clients. Whatever profession in which the client works, ask the client if he or she belongs to an association within that profession. They may be in need of your services or product.

Case in point:

Lynn Armstrong of L.A. Enterprises, a specialty advertising company, practices looking past a client's business life. Armstrong realizes that although she may be providing award plaques to the president of a sales firm, that individual may also be the coach of a soccer team. Teams need awards, and she can provide them. If someone is not in need of her products for business use, she suggests a personal use for them, one the customer may not have considered.

She could have tunnel vision and focus only on a business contact's *business* needs, yet she sees hidden opportunities. By providing her clients with ideas for their personal ventures, her clients come out as heroes to the teams they coach or associations to which they belong. She, in turn, is considered a valuable resource for her clients' personal and business lives.

Tip #83

After Delivering What You Promised, Ask for Referrals

One good turn generally deserves another. Why is it that we forget to ask for our turn?

It is easy to assume that a satisfied client will automatically recommend you to his or her friends and colleagues. Unfortunately, this rarely happens unless you ask for the referral.

When you do a good job for someone, it's acceptable to ask for the names of other people who could use your services. Passing your name to someone else may not occur to your clients until you suggest it.

It is important to draw a fine line between asking for names, and appearing desperate for more business. If your client has no referrals in mind, do not push the issue, unless it was part of your contract.

Sometimes it is more valuable to know someone than to know everything. When you call a prospect and can say that someone the prospect knows referred you, you will have a greater chance of reaching that person.

Case in point:

Through clever negotiation and a directness rarely exhibited by others, Scott Gross, author of *Positively Outrageous Service*, gets two referrals from each of his clients. In his contracts, he includes a clause that states, "When our services are delivered as agreed, we will receive two personal referrals from the client."

He not only receives the referrals, his current clients call these people to recommend his services. A personal recommendation from a satisfied customer is a powerful selling tool. Because his referral expectations are clearly outlined in his contracts, there are no surprises after his presentations. His clients are often so pleased with his work that they provide more than two referrals.

Tip #84
Follow the 13-13-12-12 Cold Call Plan

Sales is a numbers game. The more calls you make, whether in person or by phone, the more you increase your chances of closing the sale.

No one likes to hear the word "no," much less feel the anguish of rejection. Unfortunately, it's a part of day-to-day business that we all eventually face. The flip side to this agony, after a while, appears as a few yeses.

Determination, hard work and persistence always pay off. It's the waiting for the payoff that can distract you. Developing a persistence plan and playing the numbers game will keep you focused and ready to turn any weak "no" into a solid "yes."

Case in point:

With the odds in his favor, Joe Charbonneau, president of Presentations Inc. and a master speaker, plays a numbers game to increase his sales. He knows that although he would like to, he and his staff will not close every sales call they make. To increase his company's closure rate, he devised a comprehensive sales method that he calls the "13-13-12-12 plan."

Charbonneau relies on frequency of calls to different prospects to keep his calendar filled with over 200 speaking engagements each year and his business account bulging. His plan starts on Monday. Make 13 contacts by phone. Leaving a message or faxing information without talking to someone first does not count. You must make 13 voice-to-voice contacts.

On Tuesday, make another 13 contacts and, on Wednesday and Thursday, make 12 contacts. Charbonneau has a policy that no information is sent until the end of the day. He wants everyone in his office to maintain their momentum and keep dialing. In addition, no information is sent until someone in his office has had a conversation with the person requesting the information.

Charbonneau's company averages two sales for every 50 calls. His profits far exceed the time spent calling and the dollars spent mailing and printing sales materials.

Tip #85

Sell Magic Moments

Do you remember the feeling you had when you bought your first car or first home? To others, your purchase may have appeared as a heap of metal, vinyl and rubber, or bricks, boards and cement. To you, your purchase represented the culmination of years spent scrimping, cutting corners and doing without to make this car or house a part of your life.

Wouldn't it be nice if everyone who bought your product or paid for your service felt the same way about your product or service? They can, but it's up to you to paint the picture for them.

Describe, in detail, how your service or product will benefit the client—whether it's the feeling of self-confidence after a beauty makeover with your company's products, or a future of leisure and relaxation when your clients allow you to handle their retirement planning. Certainly you want to share the virtues of your service, yet every potential client wants to know what's in it for *them*. If you take people beyond the product and sell the feelings behind it, you will be offering something they just can't resist.

Case in point:

By bringing out the feelings associated with his products, Jim Halt, sales consultant for Jostens, sells award after award. He is not only selling plaques, awards and other ways to express recognition, he is providing "magic moments."

Halt wants to do more than sell an engraved tribute to someone. He wants to provide others with the tools to invoke emotions from those who receive his products.

When Halt works with a client who has no idea of what he or she wants or needs, he shares "magic moments" from other clients. He tells how awards presented to a group of sales managers boosted their morale and, ultimately, their sales figures. Another client presented "thank-you" awards to his sales staff on Valentine's Day instead of giving away the traditional turkey at Christmas. These magic moments inspire his clients to create their own special moments by using his products.

Tip #86
Send 'Love Letters' to Prospects

Testimonials provide a powerful selling tool. You can spend hours telling a prospect about your services and why they should hire you, or you can provide them with solid evidence. When someone hears about your abilities from someone other than *you*, that recommendation carries more weight.

Turn over the task of selling yourself to prospects— have your satisfied customers do it for you! Just provide prospects with reference letters. When you receive a glowing letter, share it with others, especially prospects. If you have not received a letter, yet know that your clients are pleased with your work, don't be afraid to ask for a letter.

If your clients are not willing to share their satisfaction with others, you need to reevaluate your working relationship. This is the ideal opportunity to investigate whether your clients are indeed happy with your services. If not, now is the time to rectify the situation.

Case in point:

Quality customer service is the mission of Scott Gross, owner of T. Scott Gross and Company. As the author of *Positively Outrageous Service* and *How To Get Positively Outrageous Service*, Gross knows the value of letters of recommendation, or what he calls "love letters."

When Gross sends his press kit to prospects, they see on the first page a "love letter" from his top client. He realizes that these letters say more about his company than he ever could. He recommends going as far as reproducing the letter in full color, using the colors on the client's letterhead.

Before reproducing your testimonial letters, ask your clients if they mind being included in your sales packet. Your prospects may call your clients to get more information about your abilities. If you or they prefer that your prospects don't call, delete the address and phone number from the copy of the letter.

Set up a filing system for your greeting cards. Label a hanging folder, "Greeting Cards" and the interior (manila) folders "Birthdays," "Anniversaries," "Babies," "Thank You," "Sympathy" or any other occasion for which you send cards on a regular basis. When you have cards readily available, you are more likely to send them on time. Otherwise, you may be too busy to run to the store to buy a card and, when you finally do, it may be too late. After your system is set up, buy cards in quantities. Take advantage of card sales and going out of business sales. Not only will you save money on greeting cards, but you will have cards when you need them.

Tip #87
Acknowledge, Don't Attack, Your Competition With 'Like/Unlike' Presentations

Think back to a sales presentation when you made all of your points, demonstrated the value of your product or service and were ready for the close when your prospect asked about your competitor. Your options were to ignore the question, condemn your competition or remain professional and find a method to stress the benefits of your product, without criticizing your competitor. Believing in your product or service is admirable, yet your faith shouldn't blind you to what your competitor has to offer.

You could do this without diminishing the value of the products your clients are currently using. How you react to what your clients say about your competitors could improve your relationship with your clients or do irreparable damage.

Case in point:

By being aggressive, yet sensitive to his clients' feelings, David Kessler, institutional managed-care specialist for Boehringer Mannheim (pharmaceuticals), maintains a strong rapport with his clients. Daily, Kessler talks with physicians who use his competitors' products (as well as some of his), yet he knows that if he condemns the products these physicians are using, he may insult them.

Kessler strives to make each sales call a positive one and avoids any negative statements. He does so by using a "like/unlike" method. When a physician mentions a product that Kessler's company does not sell, Kessler compliments the physician on his or her choice and compares or contrasts his product. "Like that product, mine does this..." "Unlike that product, mine does this..."

Kessler realizes that if someone is using a certain product, he or she must like it. Kessler needs to respect these choices. By using his "like/unlike" method, he is not criticizing his competitors' products. Instead, he is stressing the benefits of his products while maintaining respect for his clients' preferences.

Tip #88

Pick Low Fruits

Setting your sights on a large client with an unlimited budget is admirable, yet often time-consuming. You can wait a year for a large prospect to make a decision, only to discover that a change in management or a further delay postpones that opportunity. While searching for that client at the end of the rainbow, don't ignore the pot of gold in front of you.

During that waiting period, seek out clients with smaller budgets who are ready to do business with you. Alone, they may not boost your profits. Yet combined with others, they may help increase your profits considerably.

Case in point:

There are "golden apple" prospects and "lower fruit" prospects. Realizing that "golden apple" clients will always be at the top of the tree, Robin Johnson, a partner in Vidalia Associates, reaches for the ones that are easy to pick, or the "lower-fruit" clients. She knows that eventually the golden apple prospects will evolve into clients, but they take longer to ripen.

Johnson categorizes lower-fruit clients as decision-makers who are ready to buy and have the authority to commit to a contract. They have a budget available and meet the profile of what she and her partner are looking for in a client. In addition, these lower-fruit prospects have problems that her firm has the expertise to solve.

The beauty of lower-fruit clients is that they are easier to close and take less time to do so. Johnson obviously welcomes more golden apples to her burgeoning client list. However, as she waits for them to make a decision about her firm, she stays busy with the lower fruits and maintains her profits.

Tip #89

Anticipate Your Clients' Needs

You don't have to be psychic, although it couldn't hurt, to gauge your clients' thoughts and concerns. Some people use intuition, while others use a more direct approach: they simply ask for the information they need.

Of course, clients won't always tell you what they're thinking, so you have to determine their thoughts and feelings in other ways. What is their stance during your meeting? Are your client's arms folded across his or her chest and is he or she leaning away from you? Or is he or she leaning toward you, hanging onto every word you say?

Some clients are skilled at making "poker faces" and will never give you an inkling of what they're thinking. At that point, rely on your gut feelings and your business sense and simply ask your client what you need to know. If you ask the same question, rephrased differently each time, yet are careful to avoid annoying your client, you should get the information you're missing. Even if your client still avoids the question, the way he or she responds to the questions, both verbally and physically, may provide you with insight.

Case in point:

Carefully studying his clients' next moves is second nature to Jim Halt, a sales consultant with Jostens. He watches his clients' eyes, ready at any moment to close the sale. While anticipating a client's needs, Halt uses many tools—his intuition, their eyes and body language and direct questions. Halt asks clients what quantities they are considering for their next order, when they would want it and, more importantly, their budgets.

Halt recalls one client who was reluctant to answer questions regarding his budget. When Halt convinced him that the information would be used to help him, rather than used against him, the client disclosed the information. The client didn't want Halt to inflate prices to meet the client's budget. Halt quickly put his fears to rest and has maintained a long-term relationship with the client.

In this age of fax machines, modems and voice mail, Halt realizes that people can become more insulated, making it harder to meet with them face to face. When he can't see clients in person, Halt relies on his intuition and experience to know when to ask questions.

Does your correspondence lead to misunderstanding?

Simplify everything you write. When a two-paragraph memo or letter will do, stop there. No one wants to read anything filled with unnecessary information.

Strive to educate rather than impress. Instead of using a word that no one knows or uses, find another word. If they don't know what you're saying, why say it?

Tip #90

Interview Your Customers' Customers

When you think about it, who other than you and your staff knows more about the way your company operates, from its sales department to customer service, than your clients? Researching your clients for the purpose of improving your service to them may involve talking to your clients' departments and staff members. They often will give you a clear picture of your client, and in some instances, a clearer picture than you may want.

Talking with key people within your clients' organizations is one way to find out what makes them tick. Take it one step further and probe deeper by talking to others who know your clients well—*their* clients.

Case in point:

A bit of detective work, combined with a reporter's curiosity provide Barry Farber, author of *State of the Art Selling,* with a powerful research tool. He goes straight to the source and interviews those who do business with his clients. During taped interviews, he asks them about their business, what is important to them, what their needs are and what more they expect from his client's company.

Farber sends the tapes to his clients. By listening to these tapes, his clients gain valuable insight into their customers' needs. The information provides them with knowledge about their sales reps to determine if what they are doing is effective.

Farber, in turn, uses the information to further customize presentations for his clients. He provides them with the skills they need to improve their business and he has the facts to back up his recommendations.

Tip #91

If Your Smiling Face Is Not In Front of Your Customers, Someone Else's Will Be

---

When you assume your clients are happy and will always work with you, no matter what, make sure that you, not your competitors, are the one making your clients smile.

The steady growth of your client base will ultimately mean less time to spend with individual clients. It is imperative that you make an effort to keep in touch with clients as much as possible, without being a pest. You don't have to be face-to-face with each of your clients every day. However, making a concerted effort to stay in touch will increase the likelihood that your clients will think of you before your competitors.

Case in point:

Keeping in touch with her clients on a regular basis is Lynn Armstrong's forte. She knows that her company, LA Enterprises, is not the only specialty advertising firm in town, yet she wants to be the first one anyone calls for premium items.

Whether she is sending a client a recent article of interest to them or handing out pens, coffee cups, or other items her company represents, her clients do not feel neglected. Armstrong makes it a point to let them know she is always available to them.

Tip #92
Keep In Touch
Without Being a Pest

No matter how well you do your job, or provide a service that helps your clients achieve overwhelming success, your clients will eventually forget you. You can call your clients and risk wasting their time or take a soft-sell approach to remind your clients that you still exist.

Case in point:

David Morgenstern, president and creative director of Morgenstern and Partners, an international advertising creative service, turns completed projects into marketing opportunities. After he finishes a project, he finds a postcard that fits the theme of the campaign and sends it to 100 clients and prospects.

For example, when he completed a project for a law firm, Morgenstern sent a postcard with Raymond Burr on the front and the announcement of the project on the back to his clients.

These postcards that he mails four times a year tell Morgenstern's clients and prospects what types of accounts he handles. It reminds his clients of what he has done for them in the past and tells his prospects what he could do for them in the future. Morgenstern not only mails the postcards to his contacts within each company, he mails them to his contacts' bosses and other department members. In addition to the postcards, Morgenstern mails his clients Christmas cards and calls his clients at least once each year.

Old habits don't have to be hard to break.
Clearly identify the habit you want to break.
List the obstacles that keep you from changing.
List the steps necessary to change this habit.
Take each step, one at a time.
Reward yourself each time you make a positive change.

Tip #93

Be a Super-Sleuth

Any good detective knows that to uncover the truth, you have to dig for the facts. In business, as in crime, the truth may be right in front of you. All that you have to do is be willing to search for it.

Case in point:

Fact-finding is such a large part of her business that Robin Johnson and her partner named their market research and strategic communications consulting firm Vidalia Associates, after the Vidalia onion. They equate what they do with the act of peeling away the layers of an onion, searching for what's inside.

Some consultants might spend a majority of their time questioning senior management and ignoring employees below them. Senior management may not realize that many of them have been away from the "front line" for years and no longer have a grasp of the situations their people face daily. Not Vidalia Associates. They conduct one-on-one interviews and focus groups with the various levels in a company to unearth the hidden bugs in their clients' operations.

Their "investigation" starts with senior management and includes research about the company's vision. Sometimes, Vidalia Associates' job is to find out why the rest of the company does not share its leader's vision.

With that knowledge in hand, they are able to dig for clues as to how they may turn the situation around.

After reviewing their clues and the other information they have gathered, they are able to deduce the problem and devise a plan of action. Whether it is a lack of communication, internal or external, or an incongruent message, their fact-finding mission leads them to the perfect solution.

Tip #94
There Are No 'No See's,' Just 'Selective See's'

Gatekeepers may not be the barrier between you and a client. Instead, the actions of others in your industry may cause a prospect to reject yours and others' requests to meet with them in person. Your product or service may be of better quality than someone else's, yet if a prospect has had several bad experiences with your competitors, everyone may suffer.

You can accept the fact that various prospects will not budge and may continue to ignore you, or you can work to find ways to enter the "guarded walls" of your prospects' offices.

Case in point:

Institutional managed-care specialist David Kessler often goes where no man or woman has gone before—inside the offices of those who say they never meet with anyone. How does he do it?

Kessler is able to see physicians other pharmaceutical representatives have deemed "no see's," because he finds ways to help the physician's business, instead of focusing on merely selling a product. He speaks with the receptionist and nurses and asks how he may offer to provide articles or information about his products. Also, he always asks them when it would be a good time to meet with the nurses or physicians.

When Kessler is meeting with the physician, he answers the physician's questions, and if he or she asks Kessler something he does not know, Kessler searches for the answer after the appointment and lets the physician know the answer as soon as possible.

After he has met with a client, he does a "post-call analysis" to review what he covered and what he will discuss during the next meeting with a physician. The next time Kessler meets with a physician, he "advances the sale" by recapping what they discussed before.

Kessler is never deceptive in his selling techniques and respects both the nurses' and physician's time. He knows the consequences of wasting someone's time, even once. Doing so could minimize Kessler's chances of seeing either physicians or nurses the next time he visits an office.

If Kessler has nothing new to discuss, he will not meet with a physician until he does have something to cover. Meeting with a client and having nothing to share could be more detrimental than waiting another month to meet with the client.

Tip #95

Ask Customers and Prospects If They Are 'AM-ers' or 'PM-ers'

Some people are morning people, while others are unable to function until mid-afternoon. When dealing with a customer or prospect, find out if that person is more responsive in the morning or afternoon. In the past, you may have lost a sale because of the time you called.

Studies have shown that people are more responsive on certain days of the week. For example, Monday morning is not a good time to make a sales call because people often take longer to get started, or use that time to plan for the week's activities. Wednesday is a good day to call prospects and clients because the weekend is just around the corner.

By taking the time to find out your clients' and prospects' ideal times of day, you are being both considerate and smart. Your thoughtfulness will often be rewarded with a sale.

Case in point

Asking his clients whether they are "AM-ers" or "PM-ers" is a preliminary step in Jim Halt's sales process. Throughout his 21 years as a sales consultant in the recognition division of Jostens, he has figured out what works and what flops. He found that even if a prospect is interested in Halt's product, the prospect will not be as responsive in the morning if that is not his or her ideal time of day.

One time, after a client had placed an order for company awards, Halt dropped by the client's office to thank him in person. When he walked into his new client's office, Halt saw the bags under the man's eyes and told him he would be back that afternoon. When he returned, his client looked like a different person. He was alert and the bags were gone. From that point on, Halt never called on that client until late afternoon.

Are you giving your time away?

Instead of driving from place to place, looking for what you need, call ahead and ask. You will save time and gas.

Visit places at off-peak times. A one-minute phone call asking for those times could save you an hour of waiting in line.

Confirm appointments the day before. Your client may have forgotten to cancel with you.

Get clear directions before you get into your car. If the person with whom you are meeting is unsure, ask someone else in their office for directions.

Tip #96
Clearly Define Terms of Business With a Contract

A handshake and a "gentleman's word" used to suffice in business. As our society has become more litigious and business transactions more complex, a mere handshake will no longer do.

Contracts take the guessing out of business transactions and ensures that everyone receives and provides what is expected of them.

If, for example, you agree to sell your product to a distributor for a certain amount, there is never a question as to what your cost and their cost is if you include this information in the contract.

Contracts are invaluable when working with subcontractors. Clients may not know that you're farming out work, so whatever a contractor does reflects on you. A contract will help you meet everyone's expectations.

After devising a contract that all parties agree to, the next step is to enforce the terms of the contract. Otherwise, the perception of what was initially agreed upon and eventually expected may vary greatly.

Case in point:

A willingness to let her clients take the credit for making themselves look good makes Dorothy Collins, president of Organization Administrators, Inc., a hero in her clients' eyes. Her association management firm provides administrative services from managing an association's membership database to planning conferences, and takes care of tasks that various associations do not have the time or the expertise to handle.

When she started her business over three years ago, Collins was willing to do what she had to, to help a small association grow or a larger one stay focused. She learned the hard way that she needed to clearly define to her clients what was and wasn't part of her contract. If she didn't, the requests from her clients would mount and she would have little time to spend on her other association clients.

Collins wanted to build rapport with her clients, yet knew that she would have to set limitations. One of her clients hired her to manage certain aspects of their association. They were on a tight budget and decided to use volunteers within the association to oversee membership and the newsletter. Everything was fine until several members called at different times to ask Collins to help them with membership tasks that were not part of her agreement. She reluctantly agreed to help, yet realized after a few months that she was spending more time with this client than her other clients, for a fraction of the fee.

Collins eventually called the president of the association, reviewed the contract with him, and the phone calls stopped. Now, when a client calls and asks her to perform duties not included in their contract, she bills them for the extra time. Her clients receive the services they request and she is compensated for her time.

Tip #97
Offer Referral Incentives

Some clients and friends may automatically refer you to their friends and colleagues, while others need an incentive, ranging from money to products and services. There are various referral methods from which to choose.

When you meet someone who can refer business to you, you can offer to pay them a percentage of any sales you make as a result of their referrals. Then provide them with business cards and brochures or other marketing materials about your company. When you have completed a project with the referred client, pay the person who made the referral immediately. That will encourage them to refer more people to you. When you receive a call from a prospect, don't forget to ask how they heard about your company.

Another option is to provide a service in exchange for the referral. If, for example, you are a graphic artist, offer to produce marketing materials, or use your talents on another project.

Cross-promotions are another incentive for referrals. If you are doing a mailing to your clients about your products or services, include information about someone else's company. Ask the person whose marketing materials were in your mailing to do the same and include your marketing materials in one of their mailings.

The type of service and the dollar value of that service should determine which referral system to use.

Tip #98

Know How to Get Past the Gatekeepers

Businesses large and small are bombarded by sales people making presentations over the phone and in person. Personal assistants and receptionists now have to do more than type letters; they serve as barriers or gatekeepers between their employers and those who may interrupt their employers. Persistence coupled with ingenuity can make even the toughest gatekeeper hand the keys over to you.

Case in point:

David Kessler, institutional managed-care specialist for a pharmaceutical company, must meet with physicians whenever their busy schedules allow. He enjoys dealing with physicians and nurses and doesn't mind waiting for them to meet with him, as long as he is given the opportunity to talk with them in person.

Kessler knows the value of developing trusting relationships with his clients and their staffs. He realizes that no matter how well he gets along with a physician, the staff may block his path to this physician, if he alienates the nurses or receptionists in the office.

Kessler thinks of creative ways to get past gatekeepers. For example, he will make an effort to develop friendships with the gatekeepers. He may bring the office staff lunch and give a short presentation, or bring them donuts in the morning. Kessler knows that if he hasn't sold the gatekeeper on his knowledge and products, he will never be able to sell the physician on his products.

What is his secret to establishing rapport with the gatekeepers? It's simple—he treats each one with respect and avoids manipulating them. His sincerity and eagerness to improve his relationships with gatekeepers have turned them into allies instead of enemies.

On rare occasions, when all else fails, Kessler has to find ways to get around the gatekeepers. When dealing with hospital-based physicians, he finds a picture (usually posted on the wall with other physicians) of the person he wants to meet. When he passes these physicians in the hall, he stops them and asks to speak with them for a few minutes.

Tip #99

Learn to Be Quiet

When selling, the natural tendency is to extol the virtues of your product or service, dazzle a prospect with your knowledge and close the sale. Some welcome this sales approach while others find it impersonal and insulting, and close their minds along with their checkbooks.

A prospect may be initially interested in your sales pitch, yet if you do all of the talking, essentially leaving them out of the conversation, they will shut down and count the minutes until you leave or hang up the phone.

Case in point:

Being all ears is no problem for Jim Halt with Jostens, a recognition and awards company. He follows the axiom that we have two ears and one mouth for a reason—because listening is more important than talking. Halt often fights the urge to interject a point when a client is talking, knowing that he may miss a key point if he does so, and risk losing the rapport he has built with that person.

Halt thinks of himself as a reporter, searching for facts. Reporters have been using the "ask and wait" technique for years. Some of the best information they obtain comes from someone who feels uncomfortable with the silence after answering a question. Before the speaker knows it, the one big question has shed new light on a situation that the reporter may otherwise have missed.

A minute may seem to last an eternity, yet when Halt asks his prospects or clients a question, he pauses and waits for them to answer. After they respond, he waits another few seconds to see if they have anything else to say. By asking a question and patiently waiting for the answer, Halt uncovers valuable information. His clients appreciate his sales technique and show it through their orders.

Tip #100

Search the
Want Ads for Leads

Want ads have a stigma that often keeps qualified people from taking the ads seriously. After all, some people reason, if a company has to resort to the newspaper for help, the job must not be worthwhile. That is not true. The want ads offer a valuable source for leads that may direct you to lifetime clients.

There are many advantages for a business to hire a subcontractor instead of a full-time or part-time employee. The company won't have to give up office space or spend money on equipment or supplies in order to get the job done—because you'll be doing the job at home.

Another advantage is, the company doesn't have to pay for health benefits.

Case in point:

Nathan Reeder, CPA, left his employer's family-owned firm to start his own business. He knew he would need to be resourceful in order to build a solid client base. While reading the local paper, he flipped to the want ads and found the perfect way to find clients.

He answered an ad for a CPA in a medical office. When he called the number in the want ad and talked with the senior partner in the group, Reeder suggested that they hire him on a freelance basis. The physician was so impressed with the idea, and the added advantage of not having to pay for Reeder's insurance benefits, the physician hired Reeder.

Reeder worked for his first client, and still his best, for a fraction of his regular fee. He rationalized that it was better to work for a low fee that would pay for the telephone bill, instead of sitting in his office, bored, and receiving no fee. His first client continues to refer Reeder to other physicians.

Do you know when to do away with a task?

Am I constantly transferring it to the next day's to-do list?
Do I have several excuses for not completing this task?
Does something else always seem to take priority over it?
Do I know that I will never work on this task, yet keep it on my list "just in case"?

Tip #101

Develop
Ancillary Products

There are only 24 hours in each day and 168 hours in each week. Even if you could work during each one of these hours, depriving yourself of time off to sleep and eat, there would still be a limit as to how much you could bill for your time. In addition, the sleep and food deprivation would eventually get the best of you. So how do you increase your income without increasing your workload? Develop products.

Case in point:

Short of cloning himself (and if it were possible he would), Barry Farber discovered a new revenue-generating avenue for his company—books and tapes. As the author of the *State of the Art Selling* audio program and book, Farber has discovered that his "clones" are hard at work, even when he isn't.

His investment in both products was time. Developing these products took him away from his day-to-day operations, yet he knew that the payoff would be worth it. Not only do these products provide him with an additional revenue source, they expose him to people who may never have heard of him.

In addition to selling the audio program through a catalog, and his book in bookstores, Farber sells these products as a part of his seminars or makes arrangements for his clients to buy them for each of the people attending the session. The attendees hear Farber in person and use the tapes to reinforce his points.

After he published his book, he was able to raise his speaking fees commensurate with his credibility. If a company is unable to afford his speaking fees, it can buy his book and tapes.

Tip #102
Always Give More Than Expected

Although this book promises 101 tips, I'm giving you one more—it is always good to give your clients more than they expect, therefore tip number 102 is a bonus.

You can complete a project according to your contract and walk away, or go the extra mile and make your business relationship memorable.

If you're a consultant, how much does it cost you to throw in a few extra hours of consultation? If you're a freelance writer, how much time would it take you to submit a story on a floppy with the hard copy, even if the editor doesn't request it? Will a real estate agent lose money if he or she buys a client lunch in between visiting houses?

Avoid the obvious and look for unusual ways to put the icing on the cake, place the cherry on the sundae and go the extra mile (sometimes literally).

Successful Home Office Professionals Who Contributed to
101 Home Office Success Secrets

Jane Applegate
Syndicated columnist, radio commentator and author of *Succeeding In Small Business*, Los Angeles, California.

Lynn Armstrong
Owner, LA Enterprises, Dallas, Texas.

Tim Basham
President, Advertising Services and Promotions (ASAP), Austin, Texas.

Terry Brock
President, Achievement Systems, Inc., professional speaker, Norcross, Georgia.

Gene Busnar
Collaborative writer and author, Keyport, New Jersey.

Alan Caruba
Newsletter writer, editorial consultant, editor of *Power Media Selects*, lecturer and public relations counselor, Maplewood, New Jersey.

Joe Charbonneau
President, Presentations, Inc., professional speaker, Southlake, Texas.

Dorothy Collins
President, Organization Administrators, Inc.,
Deerfield, Illinois.

Mary Cowart
Independent meeting planner and owner, Mary
Cowart Meeting Consultants, Dallas, Texas.

Diana Craft
Designer/illustrator, Richardson, Texas.

Amy Dacyczyn
Publisher and author of *The Tightwad Gazette*,
Leeds, Maine.

Barry Farber
President, Farber Training Systems, Inc., co-author of
Breakthrough Selling and author of *State of the Art
Selling*, Florham Park, New Jersey.

Scott Gross
Owner, T. Scott Gross and Company, professional
speaker and author of *Positively Outrageous Service*
and *How to Get Positively Outrageous Service*, Center
Point, Texas.

Jim Halt
Sales consultant, Jostens, Dallas, Texas.

Shirley Hutton
Sales director, Mary Kay Cosmetics, Minneapolis,
Minnesota.

Robin Johnson
Partner, Vidalia Associates, Dallas, Texas.

Patricia Kaufman
    Independent insurance broker, Pompano Beach,
    Florida.

David Kessler
    Institutional managed-care specialist, Boehringer
    Mannheim, Rowlett, Texas.

Bob LeVitus
    Ccontributing editor for *MacUser* and author of *Dr.
    MacIntosh*, Austin, Texas.

Vicky Mayer
    Head, V.W. Mayer, Leawood, Kansas

Ann McGee-Cooper
    Consultant and author of *You Don't Have to Go Home
    From Work Exhausted* and *Time Management for
    Unmanageable People*, Dallas, Texas.

David Morgenstern
    President and creative director, Morgenstern and
    Partners, Los Angeles, California.

Terri Murphy
    Speaker, writer, real estate specialist and salesperson,
    Libertyville, Illinois.

John Osborne
    Business consultant, investment banker and partner,
    Osborne Applegate, Montecito, California.

Lucille Sanchez Pearson
    President, Global Resources Ltd., Rolling Hills
    Estates, California.

Laura Pedersen
Professional public speaker and financial consultant, New York

Nathan Reeder
Certified public accountant, Tool, Texas.

Art Shay
Photojournalist, Naperville, Illinois.

Sharon Sistine
Interior designer, Sistine Interiors, Beverly Hills, California.

Bill Vick
Owner of three businesses, including Vick & Associates, Plano, Texas.

ABOUT THE AUTHOR

Lisa Kanarek is a nationally recognized authority on organization and is the author of *Organizing Your Home Office For Success*. She is the founder of Everything's Organized, a Dallas-based consulting firm specializing in paper management, office organization and productivity improvement and is a sought-after speaker to Fortune 500 corporations and mid-size businesses.

Lisa is interviewed frequently by the national media and has been a guest on "Good Morning America," ABC's "Home" show and CNBC. Her regular feature, "Homework," airs nationally on the PBS program "Small Business Today." She has been featured in hundreds of publications including *The Wall Street Journal*, *Success Magazine*, *Entrepreneur*, *Home Office Computing* and *Nation's Business*. Her articles are published both nationally and internationally.

Lisa gives presentations to corporations and associations. For further information, contact:

Everything's Organized
660 Preston Forest Center, Suite 120
Dallas, TX 75230

Index